Susan Grund and other Black Widows

Ruth Kant

Published by Trellis Publishing, 2021.

SUSAN GRUND AND OTHER BLACK WIDOWS

First edition. July 12, 2021.

Copyright © 2021 Ruth Kant.

ISBN: 979-8224462131

Written by Ruth Kant.

SUSAN GRUND AND OTHER BLACK WIDOWS

RUTH KANT

Susan Grund

This is the story of a love story gone horribly wrong, and the complex web that had to be untangled to get to the truth.

The Night Of

On August 4th 1992, paramedics responded to an emergency call to Number Seven Summit Drive, Peru, Indiana. Outside, the caller still had the phone pressed to her ear, presumably still talking to Duke Memorial Hospital Emergency Room's dispatcher. Inside the master bedroom was a lifeless body lying on a couch, seemingly asleep. Upon closer inspection, E.M.T. technician Carolyn Shaffer could tell that the individual was no longer alive. There was a drop of blood on the side of the victim's mouth, and a gunshot wound through his left eye. Close behind her was Susan Grund, the lady of the house. Shaffer decided to check the pulse and the pupils of the deceased, identified as James H. Grund, just to show Susan that she did confirm that her husband was deceased. Susan kept prompting Shaffer to "do something," suggesting that they give her husband "more oxygen and some blood."

Minutes later, the house was swarming with policemen, crime scene specialists, the medical examiner as well as a few family members. This quick response by authorities was mainly because the victim was one of their own. James Grund, who was called Jimmy by practically everyone, was a third generation lawyer in the town of Peru. His death came as a shock to many, and law enforcement officers pulled into the driveway to lend a hand, and their own theories as to who could have committed the murder.

The Grund home was outside the Peru, Indiana Police Department's jurisdiction, and the case was promptly handed over to Miami County Sheriff's Department. A few moments after Sgt. Bob Land of the Miami County Sheriff's Department arrived at the scene, he placed a call to the Peru post of the Indiana State Police and requested investigator Robert Brinson to be called to the scene.

Brinson arrived at 1.07am, turning into the familiar driveway reliving the other time he had been called up to the same house. The first thing he noted was the number of people trampling all over the crime scene, with more people still pulling into the driveway. In the bedroom, Jimmy's body was on the couch, his left arm lying across his chest and his legs crossed. He had on a green golf shirt, and a Kleenex tissue was clutched in his right hand. There was a TV remote on the sofa next to him, his eyeglasses were on the coffee table, and handwritten notes were strewn about on the same coffee table. He seemed peaceful.

When he looked on the floor, Brinson immediately spotted the 9 mm shell casing that E.M.T. Paul Comerford had told him about. According to Comerford, he and Shaffer had made sure not to touch the casing, and had left it undisturbed. Also on the carpeted floor, Brinson noted, was a personal check of $295. While that part of the bedroom seemed pretty much undisturbed, the rest of the bedroom was a chaotic mess. There were open suitcases with their contents strewn all over the floor, and a look into the adjoining walk-in closet showed signs that it had been ransacked. Susan's jewelry cabinet had four drawers removed and stacked on top of each other, and Jimmy's dresser's drawers were open, his clothes partially on the floor.

Miami County Coroner, Dr. Dan Roberts, had arrived moments after Brinson, who showed him into the bedroom. After his initial examination, Dr. Roberts informed Brinson that the full examination would be carried out the next day by forensic pathologist Dr. Dean Gifford, after which he would perform the autopsy at Dukes Memorial Hospital. Crime scene specialist Dean Marks fully documented the scene, taking a vast number of pictures before switching to a video camera to ensure that nothing was missed.

As these events were unfolding in the house, other parties were doing their part to ensure that everything in this case was done by the book. County Prosecutor Wilbur Siders received a call from Kim Fenton of the sheriff's department, informing him that there had been a shooting in Jimmy Grund's home. On the other side of town, Peru Police Department Sergeant Gary Nichols noticed a sheriff's cruiser pulling up outside his home. At the same time, his phone rang, and he was informed by the Miami County Sheriff's Department to answer his door. Nichols assumed the matter was regarding a search warrant, and he was shocked to learn that his good friend Jimmy Grund had been brutally murdered. Gary Nichols promptly got in touch with Miami Circuit Court Judge Bruce Embery, and together they went over to David Grund's house to notify him of his dad's death.

Back at the house, Brinson gave the green light for the body to be taken to the hospital by the E.M.T.s. As the body was getting zipped up, County Prosecutor Wilbur Siders walked in with a search warrant for the house, signed by Judge Embrey, who had accompanied Siders to the house. While he appreciated the quick thinking on Siders' part, Brinson was starting to get irritated by all the people present in house, all of whom seemed to have an opinion on how to solve the case in seconds. So he turned his attention to the grieving widow.

After calling the paramedics, Susan Grund had called her sister, Darlene Worden, who drove three miles to the house with her husband George. The trio sat in a corner of the living room as the police continued with their initial investigation. This whole time, Susan kept telling Brinson that her husband must have interrupted a burglar. After the body was removed, Brinson asked Susan to check the bedroom and to let him know what items were missing from the drawers, suitcases and closets. Susan informed him that while some of her jewelry was missing, Jimmy's possession could all be accounted for. The scene seemed familiar to Brinson, as he had been called to the Grund's home two years prior after Susan reported a robbery. The bedroom had been ransacked in a similar fashion, and Brinson started getting suspicious about the robbery aspect of the murder. During their exchange, Brinson noted that Susan kept calling him "Bob," and he found it aggravating since they had only met a couple of times, and were not close enough for her to call him by his first name. He kept a close eye on Susan, noting that her behavior was exactly as it had been two years ago. She cried without shedding actual tears, she kept dabbing her eyes with the wet cloth in her hand, and her focus seemed to be on the mess created in the house, rather than concern for her children's and husband's welfare.

In his mind, this was an open-and-shut case. Little did he know what was in store.

Susan Sanders

Susan Grund was born Sue Ann Sanders on October 8th 1958. Shortly after her birth in Vincennes, South Indiana, the family moved to Peru. Her parents, Nellie and William Sanders, had seven children. Susan was the fourth. Her siblings were: Eddie, Rita, Randy, Darlene, Symbolene and David. They lived in the poorer part of town, and Susan grew up hating the living conditions in their home and the fact that they couldn't afford anything nice. According to Susan, her father was an alcoholic who sexually and physically assaulted her. While in second grade, her dad whipped her so bad she was sure she would die, and she suffered a severe burn on the back of her left hand. She has the scar to this day.

By the time she attended Peru High School, she was a striking brunette, and quickly became one of the most desired girls in town. At 15, she started dating Chip Groat, her first serious boyfriend. When her father attacked her again, Susan persuaded Chip's parents to let her live with them, and they agreed. It was around this time that Susan decided to change her name from Sue Ann, as she was convinced Susan had a classier ring to it. However, her relationship with Chip ended, and Susan was asked to leave the home. Going back to her parents' house was not an option for her and she drifted twenty miles away to the larger town of Kokomo.

Once there, Susan started spending time with a group of musicians. The leader of the group, Ronnie Lovell, was the lead singer of the band Mannequin. Ronnie and Lovell got married a few weeks after meeting, much to the surprise of the other group members. Susan was seventeen at the time. Ronnie was in his mid-twenties and made a living working at bars and clubs, supplementing his income with the money earned from the gigs his band played. The marriage was doomed from the start. Ronnie was unable to stay true to his marriage vows, and Susan caught him with other women a number of times. Instead of walking out on the marriage, Susan began affairs of her own. They moved to Oklahoma City, Ronnie's hometown, after he got an offer to join another band. While working as the assistant manager of the Brookwood Village apartment complex on SW 89th Street, Susan met Gary Campbell.

Gary was a trucker living three doors down from Susan's and Ronnie's apartment. Gary and Susan started spending a lot of time together, especially on those nights Ronnie was working late. That Christmas, Ronnie spotted Susan leaving Gary's apartment and asked Susan's friend about his wife's relationship with Gary. She declined to answer. When Susan got home, Ronnie confronted her, inquiring about her relationship with Gary. Susan started packing up her things, and despite Ronnie's pleas, she left and moved into Gary's place. She filed for divorce from Ronnie soon after, and she and Gary wed in the summer of 1979. At the time, Susan was pregnant with Gary's child. The marriage started out fine, and the couple seemed happy. However, Susan noticed that Gary became less interested in her after the birth of their son Jacob on June 12th 1979. During the marriage, Susan reportedly stabbed Gary twice, once with a pair of scissors and the second time with a knife. Both injuries were not life threatening, and there are no records that Gary pressed charges. However, two robberies in the house made Gary more wary of Susan. The first time, $300 went missing and Susan denied ever taking it. The second time, Gary's heirloom ring went missing and Susan denied taking that also. However, Gary spotted the ring on Susan's dad's finger and his suspicions were proven. Gary soon noticed that Susan was prone to spanking Jacob with tremendous force whenever he got her mad or irritated her. Needless to say, Gary did not recognize the woman he married.

At the time, Susan was working at the product line of Perry Filters Inc. There she met Tom Whited, the son in law of the owner of the parent company of Perry Filters. Tom had been recently widowed, and was raising his son with the help of his in-laws. Tom and Susan started an affair, and the rumors got to Gary. By this time however, he had become accustomed to his wife's infidelity. This time he realized that he was going to lose his wife after he heard that she was skipping work to meet up with Tom. After five years of marriage, Gary and Susan divorced, and Susan was given custody of their son Jacob.

In October 1982, Tom and Susan got married, and Tom's former in-laws were not invited to the ceremony. Also absent were the two children, Tommy and Jacob, who were left behind because Susan thought they would ruin the celebrations. The wedding was held in Austin, Texas, after which the married couple settled in Tom's house on Rushing Road. The house had been bought by Lester Suenram, Tom's former father-in-law and Tommy's maternal grandfather. Susan was now the parent of two sons, who had been born only three months apart. He dressed the boys in similar clothing, and even once dyed Tommy's hair to match Jacob's, much to the chagrin of Tommy's aunts and grandparents.

On January 7th 1983, Tommy was admitted to Baptist Medical Center with a swollen brain. The left temporal area of his brain was filled with blood, and an X-Ray showed a fracture on his skull. For some reason however, the police were never called to investigate the matter. When asked by a family friend what happened, Tommy said, "Mommy hit me." He did not give further details regarding the incident. On May 7th 1983, Tom got home and found Tommy throwing up. He called the doctor and Tommy was given some medication. A few hours after the doctor left, Tommy fell unconscious and was rushed to South Community at Susan's insistence, instead of Baptist Medical. As fate would have it, the pediatrician they had consulted before was not at South Community and Tommy was rushed to Baptist Medical in an ambulance. By this time Tommy was in a coma, and was diagnosed with brain hemorrhage and general brain dysfunction. Tommy had bruises on his forehead, arms, body, legs, around the rectum, and even retinal hemorrhaging. This time, hospital staff called Detective J. M. Einhorn of the Youth Bureau of the Oklahoma City Police Department.

When he got to the hospital, Einhorn was met by two hospital staff members who took him to Tommy's room. After seeing Tommy, he was convinced that he was dealing with a child abuse case. Susan on the other hand kept insisting that Tommy had an accident earlier at the supermarket. Einhorn questioned both Tom and Susan, and was having a hard time believing that the smartly dressed lady could have committed such an atrocious act. When he interviewed the hospital staff, they told him about the January incident, when Tommy had insisted that Susan was the one who caused his injuries. During Susan's interrogation, she "fainted" when Einhorn's questions became accusatory. The responding nurse quickly surmised that she was faking it. The detective then turned his attention to Dr. Richard Crook, to inquire why the police weren't called in when Tommy was hospitalized back in January. According to the doctor, "He didn't think such a responsible couple could commit a heinous act of violence on a child."

Oklahoma City Assistant District Attorney Don Deason handled the Tommy Whited case. He prepared Tom to testify against his former wife, having filed for divorce on May 18th 1983. The testimony was part of an agreement made on May 27th 1983 where Tom had been forced to submit a legal binding letter to Oklahoma City Assistant District Attorney Becky McNeese agreeing to help in the case against Susan. During the divorce proceedings however, Susan managed to manipulate Tom and his testimony kept becoming less damning. Sensing that his case was slowly crumbling, Deason offered Susan a plea. She took it. On November 14th 1983, the judge sentenced Susan to a five-year suspended sentence after pleading guilty to child beating, a felony. Tommy was placed in the care of his maternal grandparents, and Susan and Tom had their rights to the child terminated. At the time, Susan was pregnant with her second child, and she moved back to her hometown, Peru.

Susan and Jimmy Grund

Susan managed to get a new boyfriend once she got back home. However, Rick Cook lived opposite her mum's house, and she wanted more than life on the wrong side of the tracks. She kept lamenting to a longtime friend about the lack of eligible men in Peru. Her friend, George Meyers, got in touch with Jimmy's friend Gary Nichols, and the two men decided to prank Jimmy Grund.

Jimmy was recently divorced and even though he had a girlfriend, he was known to love the thrill of the chase. Nichols and Meyers set Susan and Jimmy up on a blind date, and the men failed to mention that Susan was eight months pregnant. However, the prank backfired as the two of them hit it off and soon after their relationship started, Jimmy asked his ex-wife and kids to move out of the house they had shared since the divorce. Susan moved in and their relationship seemed to flourish.

A few weeks after Thanksgiving in 1984, Susan gave birth to daughter Tanelle, and Jimmy immediately regarded her as his own daughter. Six weeks after the birth of Tanelle, the couple took a trip to Florida and got married on a boat on December 6th 1984. The marriage was witnessed by Jack Vetter, the owner of the boat. The couple came back to Peru after the wedding, and Susan finally told Jimmy about Jacob, and he set out to get Jacob back into Susan's life. However, Susan made no mention about Tommy Whited.

Jimmy started by getting Susan visitation rights, but Susan mentioned that she wanted custody of Jacob so that their family could be complete. As fate would have it, Gary had fallen on hard times and was struggling to make ends meet. Jimmy provided Gary with financial help and even moved him to Peru and got him a job. In the end, Gary transferred custody of Jacob to the Grunds, and Jimmy adopted Jacob legally and changed his paternal name to Grund. Susan then got in touch with Tom Whited, asking him to relinquish his paternal rights to Tanelle. Jimmy handled the legal aspect of the settlement, and it was agreed that the condition of the relinquishment of his rights was that he provide $25000 that would go towards setting up Tanelle's trust fund. They Grund family was finally complete.

However, despite his every intention to provide for his wife, Jimmy just didn't seem to be making money fast enough. Soon cracks in the marriage began to show, and the couple always seemed to start arguing in public about mundane stuff. Jimmy's son from his first marriage, David, was not particularly fond of Susan. This was because it always seemed like his father would give her everything she asked for and always tell David that he didn't have the money for his allowance. After living with his dad and Susan for a while, David was finally kicked out because of the frequent arguments he had with his father and he ended up moving in with his girlfriend Suzanne Plunkett and her baby Ryan. However, this relationship came with its own set of problems. Suzanne's ex-husband, Bobby Olinger, had made multiple threats against David, who finally decided to get a gun for protection. However, in his firearm application form, he listed his father's address and the permits were sent to Jimmy's house.

On July 4th 1992, Susan dropped by David's house to drop the firearm permit. Once she got there, Suzanne asked her to look after the baby while she got ready for the cookout at the Plunkett's home. It was during this time that David showed Susan the gun. Later that night when they came home from the cookout, David found the gun stolen. Nothing else had been taken.

The Investigation

Detective Brinson was having a hard time pinning down a suspect. This was because the two main suspects were not cooperating. After David Grund failed the first polygraph test, his family advised him to stop speaking to the police. He went away to school soon after. Susan on the other hand, kept finding excuses whenever she was supposed to meet up with the detective. Her actions after the murder were also suspect, but Brinson couldn't arrest the widow for not behaving in the manner deemed appropriate by society. The best lead they had so far pertained to the weapon used in the murder. Ballistics confirmed that the murder weapon was David's gun, which had just been stolen a month earlier. As to motive, the investigators were looking closely at financial motivation, especially since Jimmy had changed his will to include Susan's children as beneficiaries. However, multiple parties claimed that Jimmy had planned to change the will back to its original terms after the family trip to Alaska.

Tips kept coming in, with people informing the police about Susan's extramarital affairs, her comments about the missing gun, and most damning of all, Jimmy's plan to divorce Susan. However, police had no murder weapon and no way of proving Susan was the shooter since no gun powder residue was found on her hands after the shooting. This all changed on November 2nd 1992. Darlene Wordene, Susan's sister, approached detective Brinson outside the Miami County courthouse. They walked to the Sheriff's Department opposite the courthouse, where Brinson offered Darlene a cup of coffee and a cookie. During that meeting, Darlene told Brinson that Susan had confessed to her that she killed Jimmy. She then went on to tell the detective about Susan's strange actions after she had found out that the police had searched her home the second time. She had called Darlene and told her to ensure that nothing was disturbed in the laundry room.

Then, she asked Darlene to pick her up from Vincennes where she was staying and drive her to Peru. It was during this drive that Susan allegedly confessed to killing Jimmy. With this information, investigators decided to set up a sting operation to see if Susan would repeat the story to Darlene, and this time they were listening in. However, this was a bust. The subsequent search warrants yielded no new evidence. Despite all this, the police went ahead and arrested Susan and charged her with the murder of James H. Grund.

While Susan was in county jail, Jimmy's older children Jama and David filed legal motions contesting the validity of Jimmy's last will. They also contested Susan's claim that she was entitled to one-half of the proceeds from the sale of Jimmy's real estate. In July, the judge ruled that she was entitled to one-half interest regardless of the result of the murder prosecution. David Grund and his sister Jama Lidral filed a motion delaying the distribution of the funds. During this time, Susan's mother Nellie decided to move back to Peru from Vincennes where she had been living. When she went to her nephew's attic, she found the old metal container filled with concrete, an item she thought Susan had disposed of a while back. She took the container to Peru and handed it over to the detectives. When the concrete was scraped away, the investigators found the murder weapon at the bottom of the container.

The Trials

Susan's case was delayed several times due to various mitigating factors. First, the defense pointed out that most of the circuit judges in Peru were friends of Jimmy Grund, and this implied prejudice against Susan. They then filed a motion requesting that the case be held outside Peru, as the residents of Peru were already against Susan Grund and the jury pool would be tainted. The request was denied, but the court provided an alternative course of action. The case would be held in Peru, but the jury would be composed of people from the nearby Kosciusko County. The trial started on September 27th 1993.

In a packed courthouse, the prosecution and the defense called upon witness after witness. Darlene Worden was the prosecution's star witness, and her testimony was filled with raw emotion. Susan's mother, Nellie Sanders, also testified against her daughter. She told the court that she, Darlene and Susan had put the gun in the tin and poured concrete over it. They had then placed the tin in the attic in Susan's cousin's house, where Nellie found it later. She testified that she had assumed Susan had gotten rid of the gun, and was surprised to see it exactly where they had left it.

Susan decided to testify in her own defense. Her lawyer, Charlie Scruggs, had mentioned in his opening statement that he would prove David Grund was the person behind the murder. On the stand, Susan testified that she had been having an affair with David for years, and that he had hated his father, and wanted to "get rid of him." In his testimony, David Grund denied ever having an affair with Susan, and denied killing his father. After examining the evidence, the jury started deliberations. After fifteen hours of deliberation, they stated that they were hopelessly deadlocked, and the judge declared a mistrial.

The second trial was set for March 1994. This time around, the trial was moved to Kosciusko County Court in Warsaw, Indiana. Prosecutor Wilbur Siders was bent on correcting the mistakes made during the first trial. Charlie Scruggs, Susan's lawyer, also made changes of his own. The most notable change in the second trial was Susan's testimony. Her lawyer advised her not to mention the affair with David Grund, a decision she claims she later regretted. Her mother and sister testified against her again, and more witnesses were called to recount their conversations with either Jimmy or Susan. Perhaps the most shocking detail that was revealed was that Jimmy had apparently been planning on filing for divorce. The prosecution speculated that this was the real motive behind the murder, as Susan would receive no financial payout since she was the one guilty of infidelity. On March 23rd 1993, after thirteen hours and thirty-five minutes of deliberations, the jury returned a guilty verdict. The sentencing date was set for April 15th at 10am.

Special Judge Surbeck of Allen County sentenced Susan to forty years with an additional twenty years for aggravating circumstances. She was also fined $40,000, the maximum allowed by the law. She was then transported to the women's prison in Indianapolis. She will be eligible for parole in 2024.

HUSBAND KILLER : THE TRUE STORY OF KELLY GISSENDANER

15

JENNIFER KENDALL

Kelly Gissendaner, born Kelly Brookshire, became the sixth and last woman executed in Georgia for her role in the murder of her husband, Douglas Gissendaner, by her lover, Greg Owen. The murder was gruesome, Kelly demonstrated a lack of credibility with lies, and the murder was clearly premeditated- three things that helped a jury convict her of her role in the murder. What hurt her the most, though, was that her former lover turned on her and testified against her. Kelly seemingly changed her life in prison, mentoring and preaching to other women. Her legal team appealed the decision due to a lack of proof, her redemption, and her relationship with her children. The mother of three children cried and sang "Amazing Grace" as she received the lethal injection and one hundred people protested her death outside.

Early Life

In 1968, Kelly Brookshire was born to Maxine and Marry Brookshire in Georgia. She has a brother that was born one year after Kelly. Kelly and her brother were not born into wealth or emotional stability. Her family consisted of simple cotton farmers. Her parents drank, did drugs, and fought. Due to the troubled relationship, they did not stay together. Kelly's father left the family and created a new one with no intention of including Kelly into his new family dynamic. This obviously left Kelly feeling unwanted and abandoned. Kelly's mother did remarry a man named Billy Wade eight days after the divorce with Kelly's father was final, but Billy only added more trauma to Kelly's already broken home. Many people came forward with knowledge of sexual abuse to Kelly by her stepfather and other men. On top of the sexual abuse, Billy Wade was physically and emotionally abusive to Kelly, her brother, and her mother. Luckily, her mother also divorced Billy Wade and moved the family.

Kelly stood at six feet tall, and she was rather homely looking. Many people made fun of her for her looks and being "trailer trash". She would prefer to work rather than socialize, mostly due to her household's financial situation and her mother's strict rules. Her first job was at McDonald's. She mostly kept to herself, but the outcast made one friend in a woman named Mitzi.

First child and marriage

Kelly got pregnant with her first child before she finished high school. She claimed that the child was conceived through date rape, and the father was not actively involved in the child's life. She refused to name the father to even her best friends. She also tried to hide the pregnancy for as long as she could, but the reality became apparent around her sixth month. Before she gave birth, her father reached out to her and suggested that she name the child with his last name. Her first child, Brandon Brookshire, was born in June of 1986. Kelly married her first husband, Jeff Banks, at the young age of nineteen, but the marriage only lasted for six months before it dissolved. Reports indicate that the marriage quickly ended when Kelly's father threatened Jeff with a gun for not passing him bread at the dinner table. After the marriage ended, Kelly and her baby moved into her mother's trailer. This was a rough time for Kelly, but she was saved when she met Douglas Gissendaner.

Marriage to Douglas Gissendaner

On September 2, 1989, Kelly became Mrs. Douglas Gissendaner... for the first time. Kelly was four months pregnant on her wedding day, which could have encouraged the nuptials. The marriage was tumultuous from the beginning. They had financial difficulty after they both lost their jobs and were forced to live with Doug's parents for some time. However, Doug provided a good life for Kelly and her child when he decided to enlist in the United States Army. Despite a steady paycheck, Kelly used the money irresponsibly and needed Doug's family to help her with car payments. Doug's parents already didn't love Kelly, and this added to their distrust. When Doug moved to Germany because of his job in the army, it only added to the tension. The move happened only one month after Kelly had given birth to their first child together and her second child, Kayla. When Kelly and Doug were together, they were noticeably miserable. The relationship did not work at all, and they fought constantly. People also spoke up about Kelly's partying and sleeping around with other men while Doug wasn't around. This caused even more strain on the family, and the couple divorced in 1993. This time, Kelly joined the army with no other way to support herself and her children, but she discovered that she was not made for the army. During this time, Kelly became pregnant with another man and gave birth to her final child Jonathan who everyone called Cody. This father would die of cancer shortly after his birth. After returning from the army, Kelly and Doug reconciled. Despite having a child with another man, they didn't want to separate their family. They remarried in May of 1995 and, despite a separation during this time, bought a house together in Auburn, Georgia in December of 1996. A few months later, Doug was murdered.

Greg Owen

While divorced from Doug, Kelly started working for the International Readers League of Atlanta. At this time, she started socializing with her boss, Belinda Owens. When she met Belinda's brother Greg Owen, they had an instant chemistry. The relationship started strong, but it soon started to worry Belinda. Belinda noticed an alarming amount of fighting, and she didn't appreciate the bossy tone that Kelly used when she spoke to her brother. Kelly and Greg broke up, and Kelly went back to Doug and remarried. Kelly and Greg rekindled their romance during a brief separation between Kelly and Douglas, but Kelly ultimately stayed married to Douglas. Many suspect her devotion to her relationship with Doug involved stability for her and her children rather than love. This was only amplified by the fact that many reports indicated that she continued to maintain a relationship with Owen throughout her marriage to Douglas.

Murder and Investigation

In February 7, 1997, Douglas Gissendaner was murdered by in a secluded part of rural Gwinnett County. Douglas came home from a friend's house shocked to find Gregory Owen in his home. Gregory then exhibited a knife and forced Douglas to drive to a remote area. When they stopped, Owen forced Douglas out of the car and made him walk 300 feet into the woods before beating him in the skull with a nightstick and repeatedly stabbing him in the neck and back. When Kelly arrived, she helped set the car on fire to eliminate any evidence.

The night of the murder, Kelly had gone out for dinner and drinks with friends. Despite dancing and having a good time, she went home right around midnight. Friends with her that night reported that she told them that she went home because she had a feeling that there was something wrong. Kelly frantically searched for Doug when he didn't come home the next day. She made several calls, but she reportedly could not locate him. She even called his parents to ask if they had seen him. That same day a missing person's report was created by the local police department, and they started their search immediately.

Investigators had trouble with Kelly's story from the start. When she spoke with them, she described her marriage as happy and noneventful, but other people provided reports of fighting and numerous problems including Kelly's infidelity. One name that came up over and over again in interviews with friends and family was Greg Owen.

Greg Owen seemed to have a reasonable alibi. A roommate stated that he was home all night and got picked up by a friend for work the following morning at 9:00 a.m. With his roommate's alibi, police put Greg's interrogation on hold and continued their investigation.

Investigators finally got a big clue when they found Doug's car. It was left on a rural road in Gwinnett County. The most interesting thing about finding the car was that it appeared to be burned from the inside. At this time, there was no sign of Doug. While the situation didn't look good for Doug, family and friends knew that police were getting closer to the truth.

The day that the car was found, friends and family gathered to the home of Doug Sr. and Sue Gissendaner to support them during this difficult time. Kelly made an appearance, but she didn't stay long. She decided instead to take her children to the circus. While some people can understand how the environment can be traumatic to the children and maybe Kelly wanted to protect them, people found her decision evasive and questionable. Also, shouldn't the children be allowed to mourn with their grandparents? To increase suspicion even more, Kelly went back to work only four days into the search for her missing husband. Her behavior confused people around her. Sure, she had bills to pay, but four days was very soon to go back to work. Many people thought that she was hiding something. Many more people reported a weird attitude for a woman who had a missing husband.

After an already excruciating twelve days for Doug's friends and family, Doug's body was finally found in a horrific condition a mile from where they had found his car. His body appeared to be a bag of trash at first. He was on his knees, bent over, with his face in the dirt. Twelve days of decomposition, the elements, and animal attacks made him virtually unrecognizable. Medical professionals used dental records to confirm that the body was indeed Doug Gissendaner. He had been stabbed four times in the head, neck, and back.

While there was a long list of potential suspects, investigators kept Kelly close. When they talked to her again to go over her initial statements, the pressure must have gotten to her. She finally admitted that she had spoken to Greg on occasion when he called her. She made it clear to police that she did not pursue any relationship with Greg, and he pursued her. She also admitted that she reconciled with Owen during a separation, and she told investigators that he said that he would kill Doug when he found that she was getting back together with him. At this time, she pointed the finger at Greg and police questioned him heavily. Their relationship was officially over.

With the investigation focused on Greg, Greg's roommate changed his story completely. He was afraid that his leis could get him in trouble, and he told the police a new story. In fact, he confessed to investigators that Greg had been gone the night before until 8 am the next morning. With Greg's alibi gone, investigators knew they were getting even closer to the truth.

Kelly's story was raveling apart as well when investigators pulled up phone records that showed 47 calls between the two. They also saw that Kelly initiated the calls 18 times, which goes against what she told them while interrogated that she only spoke to him because he constantly called her. Furthermore, the correspondence ended immediately after the murder. Why would they stop talking so suddenly for no reason? Her inconsistencies made her look bad to the investigators who were suspicious of her story from the beginning.

After more interrogation, Greg confessed to the murder after he was told that cooperation could prevent him from getting the death penalty. He proceeds to implicate Kelly to save himself. He explains how he and Kelly had an intimate relationship, and she told Greg that she wanted him to kill Doug after they settled into their new house. She even came up with alibis at this time. He goes on to describe the murder in detail. He stated that Kelly picked him up and allowed her into his house. She even gave him the nightstick and the knife that he would use to attack her husband. She advised him to make it look like a home invasion and robbery. Greg waited until Doug got home at around 11 pm, and then he forced him to drive out to the boondocks by knifepoint. They eventually stopped, and Greg forced Doug out of the car and told him to walk. He committed the horrible murder by hitting him in the head with the nightstick and then stabbing him repeatedly, leaving him to bleed. Once completed, Kelly arrived with kerosene to get rid of the evidence. After the murder, Kelly told Greg that they shouldn't speak anymore until things die down. This is the confession that Greg gave police. With this confession, Greg only received a sentence of twenty five years to life instead of the death penalty.

As soon as the police had Greg's confession, they went to also arrest Kelly. They barged into her home on February 25th and completed the arrest. Kelly changed her story once again after her arrest. She confessed that she saw Greg Owen the night of the murder. This time she said that he called her, and she went to pick him up. When he picked her up, he told her about the murder. He then proceeded to threated to murder her and her children as well if she did not help him. Even though the police didn't believe her, Kelly maintained her innocence. Greg was only lying to save himself! She even turned down the plea deal offered to her and decided to go to trial. It was the same plea deal that the prosecution gave Greg- a guilty plea would give her twenty five to life, but she would not get the death penalty. Even her lawyer suggested that she take the plea deal, but Kelly decided to go to trial.

Trial

The first day of Kelly's trial was on November 2, 1998. The jury consisted of two men and ten women. Reporters were prevalent throughout the proceedings.

Prosecutors started by painting a picture of a troubled marriage between Kelly and Doug and her affair with Greg Owen. They then claimed that Gissendaner killed her husband to receive the house he bought for the family and two $10,000 life insurance policies. The reward was surprisingly small but substantial enough to be considered a motive alongside her affair. Prosecution also pointed out inconsistencies in her police reports of the night and the fact that Kelly specifically waited until Doug had bought the house for her and her children. She even had the foresight to plan alibis. This indicated that the murder was premeditated.

The prosecution brought many people into court to testify against Kelly. She faced her late husband's father, who was a witness in her trial. He brought up the troubled marriage between Kelly and his murdered son as well as her questionable relationship with Greg. While many people tried to argue that Doug Sr. already disliked Kelly, his closeness to the situation proved effective.

Another witness was Laura McDuffie. Laura McDuffie was an inmate who was in jail with Kelly. While the defense pointed out that the convict may not be the most trustworthy source and McDuffie only wanted time off of her sentence, her claims were convincing. McDuffie confessed that Kelly offered her $10,000 to take the fall for the murder of Doug Gissendaner. Kelly went so far as to provide a map and a handwritten statement of what McDuffie should say. A handwriting expert confirmed that the statement was in fact written by Kelly.

Kelly's own friend Pam was a witness for the prosecution, too. Pam told the jury that Kelly called her and told her that she had killed Doug. She called back at a later time and said that Greg had forced her to do it by threatening to kill her and her children. Pam claimed that Kelly said, "I did it,", but the defense claimed that pam heard incorrectly. Other friends also stepped up to voice they're uneasiness with her behavior while her husband was missing.

The strongest witness for the prosecution, though, was Greg Owen. His statement matched very closely with his confession, but there were certain differences that poked holes in his statement. He originally said that he drove for some time and then Kelly arrived when Doug was dead. He changed the time that Kelly showed up to the murder scene as he was finishing murdering Doug. Doug originally stated that he and Kelly burned the car together, but he then changed his story to say that Kelly simply threw a bottle of kerosene out of the window for him and he burned the car alone. Even with some holes in his original story, the confession remained very damning for Kelly. The former lovers found themselves implicating each other in their once common scheme.

The defense stated that the prosecution could not prove Kelly's innocence beyond a reasonable doubt. Furthermore, Doug Gissendaner was significantly larger than Greg and was also trained by the military. It seemed unreasonable that Doug would obey Greg's commands even if he did have a knife. Greg showed no sign of injury or struggle. It also didn't seem fair that Greg only got a life sentence when he was the one who committed the murder. Also, Greg's testimony, which was part of a plea bargain, gave him incentive to implicate Kelly for a lower sentence for himself.

In the end, a trial of her peers found Kelly Gissendaner guilty after deliberating for only two hours and sentenced her to the death penalty. In just a couple of words, Kelly's life came to an end. However, she was going to do whatever she could to save herself.

Life in Prison

Kelly was taken to prison where she was the only woman on death row. Being on death row, Kelly did her best to retain a relationship with her three children. She also continued to appeal her case, focus on her spiritual health, and mentor other prisoners.

While on death row, Kelly could not socialize with the general prison population. However, she could preach and act as a spiritual guide by talking to inmates through a vent. Mrs. Gissendaner created a bit of a name for herself in prison, and the women inmates supported her throughout her trial. They even called themselves the Struggle Sisters and rallied for her to be taken off of death row and allowed to live the rest of her life in prison.

Execution Reschedules

Her actual execution was actually the third time that Gissendaner had been scheduled for execution. She was previously scheduled for execution at the end of February, but the date was changed due to complications with winter weather. Next, she was scheduled for execution in the first week of March, but the doctors at the prison were concerned because the drug used to perform the lethal injection appeared cloudy. They sent a specimen to be tested, and, in April, they announced the results that there was nothing wrong. Gissenander's lawyers tried claiming that the changes in her execution date constituted cruel and unusual treatment, but the case was thrown out. If anything, Kelly was given more time, but her lawyers fought to the end.

Death

It was 12:21 a.m. on a Wednesday morning in Jackson, Georgia when officials declared Kelly MN Gissendaner dead from lethal injection. Her execution was scheduled for 7:00 p.m., but her lawyers attempted to repeal the decision to the very end. One hundred people stood outside of the Georgia Diagnostic and Classification Center in protest of her death. Her last meal was nachos, chips with cheese dip, and frozen lemonade.

Gissendaner showed remorse for her part in her ex-husband's death until the very end. Her last words were, "Bless you all. Tell the Gissendaners I am so, so sorry that an amazing man lost his life because of me. If I could take it all back, I would." Her words can be interpreted to indicate a sense of guilt on Gissendaner's part. It can also be interpreted to indicate a peace with her position.

Kelly Gissendaner was the only woman at death row for the entire duration of her time incarcerated, and she was the first woman to be given the death penalty in Georgia since 1945- over 70 years. She was one of only six women executed in the state, and she was the last woman to be executed in Georgia.

Appeals and Support

Kelly's lawyers made a valiant attempt at an appeal. In fact, the appeal was more than fifty pages when they turned it in, and it had statements from a number of different people, including inmates, the pope, and political figures.

After being approached by Mrs. Gissendaner's lawyer, the pope responded in a letter stating, "While not wishing to minimize the gravity of the crime for which Ms. Gissendaner has been convicted, and while sympathizing with the victims, I nonetheless implore you, in consideration of the reasons that have been presented to your Board, to commute the sentence to one that would better express both justice and mercy."

The endorsement by the pope was powerful, but the Catholic Church had also just recently vocalized a stance against the death penalty. Even former Georgia Supreme Court Chief Justice Norman Fletcher stood up for the defendant saying that her role in the murder did not constitute the death penalty. In addition to these endorsements, 90,000 people also signed a petition to support Kelly. Kelly's lawyers showed the courts that Kelly showed remorse and represented a criminal who had turned her life around to bring positivity to those around her. They argued that her presence was significantly greater than her absence to those around her, especially her children and other inmates.

Mrs. Gissendaner's lawyers attempted three appeals to the U.S. Supreme Court, but they were denied all three times. Unfortunately, on the day of the execution, Mrs. Gissendaner's children had to choose between saying good-bye to their mother or appearing in front of a judge for one last attempt to appeal her case. The last time that they saw their mother was two days earlier on Monday. In the most heartbreaking of all testimonies, Kelly's daughter, Kayla pleaded with the court to save her mother's life. She made the point that she had already lost her dad, and he would not want her or her siblings to endure any further loss by also losing their mother. Despite the emotional appear and strong endorsements, the court did not waver on its original decision.

Despite the support from multiple sources, Douglas's family, especially his father, maintained throughout the trial that they trusted the legal system and agreed with the sentence of the death penalty. They reminded the public that she chose to go to trial instead of pleading guilty. They also reminded the public that Douglas did not get any choice in what happened to his life. After the gruesome death of their son, an exhausting and emotional search for the truth, and a prolonged trial, Douglas Gissendaner Sr. and Sue Gissendaner got justice.

Death Penalty Debate

Kelly Gissendaner's case became famous across the nation because of its legal implications regarding the death penalty. People for the death penalty noted that Kelly had orchestrated the entire murder, she helped dispose of the body, she lied multiple times, and the family of Douglas Gissendaner deserved justice. People opposed to the death penalty noted that there was room for doubt, she technically did not commit the murder, the person who did commit the murder escaped the death penalty, she showed remorse over her part in the murder, she experienced trauma in her childhood, and she regularly preached and encouraged other women in the prison. Men and women all over the country debated the case, but, ultimately, the death penalty ruling was honored by the state of Georgia, and Kelly was executed while she sobbed and sang "Amazing Grace". She was 47-years-old.

ARSENIC ANNA : THE TRUE STORY OF SERIAL KILLER ANNA MARIE HAHN

DARLA PUGH

"Anna was flat broke. But when she saw a person walking down the street she would think that individual had HER money in their pocket. If she had to kill that person to get HER money, then she would take out her poison and say 'let's get this party started.'" - forensic psychologist Paula Orange

Anna Marie Hahn had a gambling habit.

She indulged her addiction at the horse races and bookie joints throughout Cincinnati in the 1930s. Anna wasn't very good at picking horses, losing time and again while accruing debt.

But it was an addiction had to be fed.

She needed a scheme, a way to acquire money to keep her compulsion satisfied.

Anna Marie Hahn was a clever woman. While walking through her neighborhood of elderly pensioners, the idea came to her like a bolt of lightning.

She would befriend these lonely and pathetic men. Cook them meals, keep them company.

Then she would kill them for profit.

EARLY LIFE

Anna was born Anna Marie Filser on July 7, 1906. She would be the youngest of twelve children born to a well-to-do Catholic family. Nothing in her childhood would suggest that she would eventually become a serial killer. She was never abused sexually or physically.

Nonetheless, she had suffered a few concussions during her childhood years during ice skating, biking and skiing adventures. These head injuries may have attributed to altering her personality as sometimes been the case of some serial killers. Anna also stated that she was a sickly child, suffering from blood poisoning, goiters, and scarlet fever. It is her belief that these instances led to "her mind changing that she could do the things that happened."

As a teen, she had given birth to a son named Oskar out of wedlock. The identity of the father has remained shrouded in mystery to this day although some claim a Viennese doctor had seduced Anna Marie.

She never revealed who the father was as he was a married man who wanted her to abort the child. Anna felt "just like a mountain was falling on top of her, not killing her but just smothering and crushing her."

The pregnancy brought shame to Anna's family. They sent pregnant seventeen-year-old to live with a sister in Holland until the baby was born.

She would return to Germany afterward and remain there for five years. The shame of being a single mom in a conservative, judgmental society would prove to be too much for Anna to bear.

"I could no longer stand those things that people were saying about my misfortune," Anna said. "I was afraid that my son would understand those things. These things were hurting my mother who was caring for my boy."

"Back in the day," Orange said. "Having a baby out of wedlock was the worst thing a woman could do in terms of family legacy. She had humiliated her entire family and was banished to another country. It certainly is an antiquated notion now, to shame a woman for having a child out of wedlock and it has become the norm. In Germany, however, this act was cause for ostracization."

Anna left Germany and arrived in the United States on February 12th, 1929. She had a step-uncle who lived in Cincinnati to whom she had written a year earlier. "I want to come to the United States," she wrote. "I'll repay you if you can lend me money for the trip. I will have little trouble finding work as a housekeeper. Please write back."

Her step-uncle, a seventy-four-year-old retired carpenter, was impressed with Anna's ability to provide for herself once she arrived. She did so well, in fact, that he became suspicious of how she acquired her money.

Oskar would stay behind in Germany with her parents while Anna would live with her now expatriated relatives Max and Anna Doeschel. Growing accustomed to the American way of life, she would meet another German immigrant named Philip Hahn at a dance. Philip was immediately smitten by the blonde and buxom Anna. The courtship did not last very long, a few weeks of dating was all the convincing Philip needed to ask Anna to marry him.

Anna agreed to marry him only on the condition that she be allowed to bring her son from Germany to live with them. Philip consented and the two were married three months after their first meeting on May 5th, 1930, in Buffalo, New York. Two months later, Anna would return to Germany and bring back Oskar who was now six years old. Philip would work as a telegrapher and do his best to now provide his new family.

Wanting a better life for her son, Anna convinced Philip that they should do more. The Depression was in full bloom but that did not stop Anna and Philip from starting their own restaurant and then a bakery. Both ventures would prove to be economic failures. The two soon became bankrupt and were forced to move in with a childhood friend of Anna's father.

Thus marked the continued humiliation of Anna. Branded as a whore by her own family, she was shunned and banished to America where she would suffer the indignity of becoming bankrupt.

GERMANS IN CINCINNATI

There was a sizable German population in Cincinnati and Anna was able to fit in and find friends. She settled in a community called Over The Rhine and she was welcomed with open arms.

She repaid some of these new "friends" by killing them.

"She had it all," author Diane Britt Franklin said. "She knew how to manipulate, steal, poison."

But what prompted her to turn to murder?

The friend of Anna's father had left his home to the Hahn's but they still had a mortgage to pay. Philip lost his job as a telegrapher, a victim of both technology and the Depression. The walls started to close in on the couple as creditors began making threats to take possession of her home.

Anna did not know what else to do.

So she turned to gambling.

Three years into her marriage, Anna was neck-deep in debt because of her gambling habit. She loved the racetracks but could never pick a winner. She would play horses at the Blade, a bookie joint in suburban Elmwood, Ohio then the gaming tables in Newport.

The addiction grew faster than her pocketbook would allow.

She needed money. Fast.

So she found a new way to "earn" money. Unbeknownst to her husband, Anna began plotting ways to pilfer money out of elderly German men who lived in Over the Rhine.

She developed a method typical of male serial killers in that she had a typical victim. Anna thought long and hard about what type of man she should target. The lonely. The old. The German, with whom she would be able to ingratiate herself to.

Anna found an apartment building in Cincinnati that was comprised mostly of older German men.

They were the perfect foil for Anna Hahn. A young and beautiful German woman who spoke their language, they easily fell prey to her charms.

"She went through apartment buildings," Franklin said. "She knocked on doors and asked for old men who were single."

"She developed a method of extracting money from wealthy old people," Orange said. "She would gain access into their homes by offering her services as a nurse. Then she would take their money."

Ernst Kohler was believed to be her first victim. Anna had befriended the lonely German man and he had willed his house to her.

Getting the sense that she was onto something, Anna began "befriending" more elderly men. The next victim was seventy-two-year-old Albert Parker who enlisted Anna's aid as a caretaker. Anna would borrow over $1,000 from Parker and signed an I.O.U for it. After Parker's death, the letter of debt "disappeared."

SETTING THE STAGE

Anna dressed her son in his Sunday's best before they went prospecting for victims. The little boy wore a brown suit with a beige shirt and a derby hat. Anna dressed conservatively, looking like a German mother taking her son out to Sunday School. She wore a gray jacket with a black silk blouse. But Anna made sure that her silver cross necklace stood prominently over her cleavage.

She then knocked on the apartment door of Jacob Wagner and put on her best smile.

Th door creaked open and the elderly German man peered out at them, saying nothing.

"Mr. Wagner," Anna said in a strong German accent. "I'm Anna Marie."

The old man's face brightened with good cheer. He had a young woman to help around the house with chores.

Little did he know that Anna would help herself to his bank account and personal belongings.

"She would take a nickel as easily as a dollar," Franklin said. "She would steal anything in sight."

Jacob Wagner was a retired gardener who only had a few thousand dollars in savings. He was targeted by Anna who would tell his neighbors that she was his niece. The old man became confused, responding back that he had "never heard of her."

"Neither Jacob nor the rest of the community fully realized what a psychopath Anna was," Orange said. "If you had something she wanted, whether it be money or material goods, she would do anything in her power to obtain it. If it meant killing you, so be it."

Anna knew that she only need to apply her feminine wiles on Wagner and he would be putty in her hands. She told the old man that she was an heiress to $15,000 from Germany. She wanted to pool their resources to buy a chicken farm but in the meantime would working around his apartment.

The seventy-eight-year-old Wagner would die on June 3rd, 1937, only months after hiring Anna. The day after the gardener's death, Anna would go to Wagner's bank and present a check that was made payable to her. The bank asked her about the death of Wagner, she had conceded that she had forged the check. Anna would not stop there. She would appear before a probate court with a will that left all of Wagner's property to her.

She had forged out a will but didn't realize that Wagner never developed the ability to write in English.

"I hereby make my last will and testament," Anna wrote on behalf of Wagner. "I am of sound mind and no influence. I have my money in the Fifth Third Union bank. I want my funeral expenses paid and all my bills. The rest I leave to my relative, Anna Hahn of 2970 Colerain Avenue, who will be the executor of my estate. I want no flowers and I do not want to be laid out. (Signed) Jacob Wagner."

She would steal his money to pay off her gambling debts. But the addiction would not go away.

Anna simply could not stop herself from gambling.

She would go to the racetracks up to four times a week and her losses once again began to accrue.

"Anna was very smart when it came to selecting the right victim and circumstance," Orange said. "But she was too stupid to realize that she wasn't very good at picking a good horse. She had a compulsive personality disorder. Anything that she saw had a positive benefit would be repeated over and over again. She became good at getting into the graces of older men and taking their money. So that became another addiction that she had to feed."

MORE LONELY OLD MEN

Anna would meet another elderly man in the mostly German neighborhood. His name was George Heis. She would arrive at his home and entertain the old man with her charm and gaiety, making drinks for him as he sat on his couch.

"Mr. Heis was a coal dealer that she met and befriended," Franklin said. "She got very friendly with him. He would take the money he would collect from his coal deliveries and give it to her."

George lived it up with Anna, drinking up the best bourbon and laughing it up in his living room.

He didn't know that Anna was counting the days when she would kill him.

One night, she would lace his drink with arsenic. He would remain paralyzed for the rest of his life.

"Arsenic loves to attack the endothelial cells," Orange said. "Those that line the blood vessels. When it attacks, those blood vessels begin to leak. Leakage of blood anywhere, particularly in that central nervous system, can cause symptoms such as paralysis."

Heis drank Anna's poisonous concoction and immediately began gasping in pain. He stood up and staggered around the room.

Anna simply watched as the old man's eyes bugged out as he tried to make it to the bathroom.

"She was heartless," Orange said. "She would watch the old man stagger in front of her, begging for help. Her only response would be to take a sip from her own drink as he collapsed to the ground and writhed in pain."

Anna would not stop with George Heis. She continued to poison men and the community was none the wiser.

"Yeah, all these people were dying in this close-knit community," Franklin said. "And no one was saying a word. Eventually, someone spoke up and said 'Hey, we're missing one.' And they reported it to police. The police didn't believe it. They didn't have any evidence to go on and they would just slough it off."

The coal company began to inquire with Anna for the money she owed Heis. She had to find a new benefactor and found one in Albert Palmer, a retired railroad watchman who had a small pension. She would meet Palmer at the Blade, the gambling joint where Anna frequented. Palmer became smitten with the youthful Anna who wrote the lonely old man love notes, calling him, "my dear, sweet Dady" (sic) and would sign her notes to him "with all my love and kisses, your Ann."

"I wrote like that," Anna said," because I regarded him like a father."

Anna would borrow money from Palmer which she used to pay off the coal company. Anna had provided company to Palmer and cooked him "homestyle German meals." Palmer was smitten by Anna but not so smitten that he didn't want his money back. Anna then took care of the debt owed to the old man by giving him a nice helping of poison in his mashed potatoes.

Palmer then became ill and died on March 27th, 1937.

CATCH ME IF YOU CAN

Anna was getting away with murder with no end in sight.

"Even today, you don't suspect a woman of being a serial killer," Franklin said. "They're not that many. But maybe there are a lot more than we think because they're hard to detect. They're very hard to detect. Who would suspect a nice German lady like Anna Marie Hahn of being a serial killer? You just would not believe it and the police didn't either."

Anna was able to avoid detection because of her ability to think rationally and plan out her attacks. Unlike some of her fellow serial killers, her murders were not done on the spur of the moment. They were cold and calculating with Anna waiting for exactly the right time to execute her victim.

That next victim would be sixty-seven-year-old George Gsellman.

Lonely and pathetic, he nonetheless jumped at the chance to have the young German beauty as his caretaker. She waited on him hand and foot, cooking his meals and cleaning up around the house. Her son would also quickly befriend the sickly Gsellman whom she was slowly poisoning with arsenic and croton oil.

Anna would use the croton oil in order to flush the arsenic out of the system. The oil would cause almost immediate vomiting and on its own could cause death if the victim is not properly re-hydrated.

Anna would take Gsellman for all that the old man had. He would eventually die alone in his room.

"Anna's appetite to get what she wanted had no limits," Orange said. "She wanted that money. Needed that money. That being said, she probably enjoyed the rush of taking someone's life. You don't do something like that for so long without a psychological payoff of some kind. Anna kept killing men not only for profit but because she liked it."

THE DEATH OF JOHANN OBENDORFER

"2150 Clifton Avenue was the home of Johann Obendorfer," Franklin said. "On street level is his little cobble shop that Anna Marie walked into one day because she had broken her heel while out shopping. He fell in love with her but she had other designs. Can you imagine how happy he must have been to have snared this beautiful woman? Little did he know that in two weeks he would be dead."

Obendorfer was the typical lonely widow that Anna would target. She entertained his affection for her by telling him that they should go to Colorado and live on a ranch.

Obendorfer agreed. Accompanied by her son Oskar, Anna would travel with the elderly Obendorfer to Colorado.

But they never bought a ranch together.

Within one day of their arrival in Denver, Obendorfer became deathly ill in his hotel room after Anna gave him some food. He was taken to Bethel Hospital and Anna registered him as being from Chicago. "I didn't have any money," she said. "I didn't want to be responsible for any bill."

"By the time they got to Denver," Franklin said. "Mr. Obendorfer had gotten very, very sick. She had been poisoning him the whole trip."

She would deny knowing Obendorfer to the hospital staff. They inquired for some identification of the man and Anna leaned over her benefactor on his death bed.

"Old man," Anna said. "Tell these people your name. Tell them who you are."

Obendorfer could not even manage a whisper, he was so weak.

"I don't know who he is," Anna said, throwing her hands in the air. "He's just an old German that I met on the train."

Anna then left the hospital and felt that she wanted more out of the trip that what she was stealing from Oberdorfer. Prepping to leave town, she had one more heist in mind.

"The hotel owner had rooms right behind the registration desk," Franklin said. "One day Anna Marie walked right into one of those private rooms. She saw two diamond earrings on the dresser and stole them. When the hotel owner realized they were missing she filed a complaint with the police in Colorado Springs. By that time Anna Marie and her son had left town and left poor Mr. Obendorfer on a slab in the morgue."

An autopsy would reveal high levels of arsenic in Obendorfer's body.

While Anna was away in Colorado Springs, the police in Cincinnati had finally become suspicious of Anna. They searched her house and found some incriminating evidence.

The police would search through one of her purses and find a salt shaker with enough arsenic inside to kill off all the inhabitants of a small town. They also found a bottle of croton oil that was marked with the words "poison." They found a bottle which contained more than seventy grams of arsenic lodged between the rafters between the cellar and the first floor.

Upon returning home, Anna would be confronted by the police. They would interrogate her about the poison and Anna would deny ownership of the contents but want it back nonetheless.

The police chief at the time, a man named Hayes thought that his intimidating questions would force Anna to crack under pressure.

"There are an awful lot of men dying around you, Mrs. Hahn."

"I love to make old people comfy," Anna said. "It isn't my fault that all these old men are dying. I know it is very peculiar, but why pick on me, Chief?"

"We searched your place, Mrs. Hahn," Hayes said. "We found enough poison to kill half of Cincinnati."

"I have been like an angel of mercy to them. The last thing that would ever enter my head would be to harm those dear old men."

TIGHTENING THE NOOSE

Anna would visit a physician named Dr. Vos whose office was in a building Annie owned and occupied. The doctor would soon discover that many of his blank prescription forms were missing. Anna's husband Philip would come forward with a bottle of poison and inform police that Anna had, in fact, stolen the prescription forms. She would forge the doctor's signature and order the poisons from the local pharmacist.

"She would send our twelve-year-old son, Oskar, to get the prescriptions. One pharmacist refused to fill the prescription because of the boy's age."

Philip then told police that Anna had tried twice to insure his life for $25,000 but he had refused to sign off. After his refusal, Philip began to become ill with the same symptoms as some of Anna's previous victims.

Philip's mother demanded that she take her son to the hospital where it was revealed that he was being poisoned. He recovered but never spoke to his wife again.

With the evidence provided by Philip the police now had enough to arrest Anna Marie Hahn.

On August 10th, 1937, Anna would be placed behind bars.

"She got too cocky," Orange said. "She would leave behind too many clues, in particular with Obendorfer. She forgot to cover her trail and the police eventually got her on their radar. The irony was that the predator, Anna, now became the prey of the police as they spent months gathering evidence on her."

Anna would plead not guilty to the charges of murdering Gsellman. She claimed that she didn't know the man. But a friend of Gsellman told the police that they had witnessed Anna visiting the old man the night before he died.

The investigation grew in scope as the deaths of five other old men and another couple had all died without warning but with one thing in common.

They all were friends of Anna Marie.

THE TRIAL AND EXECUTION

"It took me a long, long time to find that it is wrong to be good to people," Anna said to a reporter outside her trial. "This doesn't mean I am going to be hateful from now on because that is against my nature. They can take a human's body, but they can't take their soul because that will go where there is justice."

When her case went to trial, it shocked a nation that had never seen a female serial killer before.

During the trial, newspaper reporters described Anna as "poker-faced, blonde German woman who at no time displayed any appearance of resentment or shock at anything that has been said."

The prosecutor in the case spared Anna no mercy.

"In the four corners of this courtroom are four dead men," he bellowed. "These men are pointing their bony fingers at this woman as they say, 'That woman poisoned me. She made me die in agony. She made me suffer the tortures of the damned. Let my death not be in vain."

The defense attorney argued back that the evidence against Anna was circumstantial and that she was a "victim of a cruel sequence of coincidence."

"What was shocking to everyone," Franklin said. "Was that the jury returned a verdict of guilty without mercy."

The jury would be comprised of eleven women and one man. The prosecuting attorney felt that if the jury was comprised of a male majority they would see Anna as a sympathetic figure. So they stacked it in favor of females.

The guilty verdict meant that Anna would be the first woman in Ohio history to be sentenced to death in the electric chair.

Anna still had enough charm and wit to play on the sympathy of people.

"The judge cried," Franklin said. "Because he had to sentence Anna Marie to death. He had no choice."

"At the end of the day, Anna proved to be like most every other serial killer," Orange said. "She thought that everyone else was beneath her in terms of intelligence. They don't think they can be caught and the vastly underestimate the scope and IQ level of the people around them which include the police. Anna thought she was more cunning that everyone around her. For awhile, she was. Then the noose tightened around her neck and she had nowhere to go."

The night before her execution, Anna would sit down and write out a twenty-page confession of all of her murders. She tearfully described every detail in the small journal, addressing it to "Dear Lord."

"On one hand, you can look at her confessional as a letter begging for forgiveness," Orange said. "But women like Anna aren't remorseful without a payoff. Cold and heartless, she wanted to remain in control until her final breath. Her confessional letter was yet another attempt at control. She wanted to be in charge until the very end."

"I do not show my feelings," Anna wrote. "My troubles in life, starting when I had my baby, had taught me how to control my feelings...I don't know what made me do it. All that I can say is that my troubles were so big that it must have turned my mind. I do not try to excuse myself or my actions. They were not me at all...It all seems like a horrible dream...I wanted to cry out that they were trying the other Anna Hahn and not this one sitting in the courtroom...Maybe it would have been different if I had only told my lawyers the truth. My lawyers fought so hard for me. But that is all over now...I do not fear my end and my last concern is only for my boy. I have written this confession with the full knowledge that death is near and I only ask one favor and that is that my son should not be judged for the wrongs that his mother may have done."

The sale of Anna's confession to the newspapers allowed Anna's attorneys to take care of Oskar's future. They moved him away from Cincinnati and had him placed under a new name. Her husband Philip would remarry shortly after the trial.

There are competing reports of how Anna behaved as she waited to be executed. Some reports describe her as pleading to see her son for one last time. Others describe her as mocking that report, sarcastically asking "do I look like someone who is distraught?"

Nonetheless, before being executed Anna pleaded for mercy. She had reached out to Ohio Governor Daley to grant a stay of execution.

"This was one of the most difficult decisions I've ever had to make," Governor Davey said. "Something inside me sort of rebelled against the idea of allowing a woman to go to the chair but the crimes committed by Hahn were so cold-blooded, so deliberately planned and executed that I have no choice but to permit the decision of the court to stand. I feel sorry for her son, Oscar, but his mother has bequeathed him nothing to be proud of."

Anna would be sent to the electric chair on December 7th, 1938 at the Ohio Penitentiary in Colombus, Ohio. She refused to see her husband and son on the last night of her life but allowed reporters covering her trial a farewell party. Several of the newsmen entered Anna's cell. She had fruit punch and cake prepared for them.

"You gave me a 'good show' at my trial, boys," Anna said. "The least I could do was to throw a bash for you. I guess I'm not much like a 'beautiful blonde' now, huh? Well, give me a good write-up when it's all over."

THE ELECTRIC CHAIR

"Don't do this to me!" Anna screamed at the prison attendants who began strapping the electric belts to her leg. She writhed against the grip of the guards as they held her down, strapping her to the chair.

Anna screamed in mercy. A priest entered the room just as the black death mask was placed over her head. Her screams and pleas became inaudible.

"Our Father, who are in heaven," the priest said.

Anna could be heard repeating the prayer until the execution flipped the switched as the heavy jolts of electricity crackled through her body.

She screamed for mercy then continued the Lord's Prayer.

"But deliver us-"

Those were her final words.

It took two and a half minutes to kill Anna Marie Hahn on the electric chair.

"Did she protest her innocence to the last?" a news reporter asked her attorney, Joseph Hoodin.

"I won't comment on that," Hoodin said.

"But did she admit her guilt?"

"I understood the question," Hoodin said. "And I still won't comment."

Anna would be buried at the Mount Calvary Cemetery in Cincinnati, Ohio.

HUSBAND KILLER : THE TRUE STORY OF AUDREY MARIE HILLEY

45

ANNA DELANEY

Audrey Marie Hilley

"That woman was pitiful," said Janice Hinds, 50, one of two neighbours who called police and cared for Hilley after spotting her sprawled on the deck of Thomason's home.

"We didn't know she was Marie Hilley. She didn't look like Marie Hilley," said Hinds, who grew up in the same Blue Mountain cotton-mill town as Hilley. "Marie Hilley was a sophisticated lady. She had pride in her looks, her dress."[1]

Her Early Life

Audrey Marie Hilley was born on June 4th, 1933 in Blue Mountain, Alabama. Her parents, Huey and Lucille Frazier, worked hard at the Linen Mill to provide for their family, and Marie (as she was known) was often looked after by relatives when her mother returned to work shortly after she was born.

Huey and Lucille loved their only child but showed their love with material things rather than affection and time. She was always well-dressed and had nice things, and as a result, Marie became rather spoilt. She was well known for her temper tantrums when things didn't go her way, and her parents, possibly out of guilt for not being there, rarely checked her for her behaviour.[2]

The Fraziers were proud people and were determined that their only child would not spend her life working in the same mills as they, and most of the town's inhabitants, had always done. They wanted more for their daughter and instilled in her an ambition to be a secretary, a lofty ambition for someone from a mill town.

In 1945, the Fraziers moved from Blue Mountain to Anniston, and Marie enrolled at Quintard Junior High School. Anniston was a whole new world to the girl who had felt she was above the rest in her old hometown. Marie went from being a big fish in a small pond to a small fish in a much more upscale lake, and for the first time in her life found herself at a disadvantage. In Anniston, all the girls wore nice dresses and what was more, some of their parents were the owners of the same mills that Marie's parents worked at.

Marie threw herself into her studies, making a name for herself as a diligent, intelligent student, and she integrated herself into new social circles – her friends were from privileged families and Marie wanted to be a part of that.

It wasn't just the teachers for whom Marie stood out, though. She was also a pretty girl and had her fair share of the attention from the boys, too. In fact, by the end of the 7th grade of Junior High School, Marie Hilley had been voted the prettiest girl in school by the yearbook staff.

It was around this time that 16-year-old Frank Hilley noticed 12-year-old Marie, and by the time he graduated High School, he was in love.[3]

Frank and Marie

In contrast to the Frazier family, who loved their daughter but showed no affection, Frank Hilley's family was warm and affectionate. The Hilleys worked in the other big industry of the area – pipe making - and even though they did not have much money, Clarence and Carrie Hilley made a happy, comfortable home for their three children – Frank, Jewel and Freeda.

Marie's parents did not approve of Frank – he was not from one of the affluent families of Anniston and Huey and Lucille wanted more for their daughter – but Marie was happy to be Frank's girl, and in return, he treated her like a princess.

Frank joined the Navy after finishing High School and was assigned to Guam but the distance between them bothered Frank. He was worried that with him so far away, and with so much time apart, Marie might find someone else so, on May 8th, 1951, before 17-year-old Marie had even finished High School, the young couple married.

Married Life

Marie remained in Anniston to finish her education and then joined Frank in Long Beach, California before the couple moved to Boston where Frank finished his stint in the Navy. It was while they were in Boston that they discovered Marie was pregnant with their first child, and the couple moved back to Anniston and bought a small home. Frank secured a job with a local foundry, and Marie found work as a secretary. Like all couples, the pair had their ups and downs, but for the most part, they seemed happy.

Their first child, Michael Hilley, was born on November 11th, 1952.

The Troubles Begin

Marie had been brought up to want the best of everything. While Frank was still in the Navy he had sent all of his paychecks home to his young wife, and yet when the time had come for her to join her new husband in California she had no money to pay for the journey. She had been spending his wages without telling him, and his parents had had to finance Marie's travel in order for her to join her new husband.

Despite the extra financial burdens having a young baby places on a family, Marie's spending didn't decrease. She wanted nice clothes and expensive home furnishings, and Frank, not liking to upset his wife, gave in to her, just as her parents had when she was a girl. Marie was a woman who was used to getting her own way.[4]

In 1959 Marie's behaviour began to become more sinister. She started taunting Frank, waving love letters she said were from other men in front of him but not letting him read them. She would then leave the torn up pieces where her husband could find them. Frank pieced them together, and it became clear that his wife had written them herself. When he confronted her she said she was afraid he didn't love her anymore and wanted to make him jealous.

By this time, Marie was spending double her take-home pay from her own job on fine clothes and luxuries. To prevent Frank, who was extremely responsible financially, from finding out she would get up early in the morning to check the mail and hide the bills.

Marie became pregnant again, and on January 14th, 1960 she gave birth to a baby daughter, whom they named Carol Marie.[5]

Carol

By the time Carol was born, things should have been looking up for the family. Frank had been promoted at work, and Marie had developed a reputation as a first class executive secretary. However, as the family's income rose, so did Marie's spending. Furthermore, she was becoming known for a peculiar situation at work. While her bosses loved her for her politeness and diligence, her co-workers greatly disliked her. They found her to be very judgemental of those around her and felt that she put on airs and graces and acted as if her co-workers were 'beneath' her. When she became disliked she would leave, and complain to friends and family that her colleagues had 'ganged up' on her and driven her from her job. Her employers, though, always gave her exemplary references, and she never found it difficult to get another job. In fact, Marie Hilley worked for some of the most powerful and affluent men in Anniston.[6]

Marie was disappointed with her daughter, Carol. She wanted her daughter to wear pretty dresses and have bows in her hair, while Carol was more of a tomboy and would often go to football games with her father. The pair developed a close father/daughter relationship and Marie was deeply resentful and jealous. She lamented the fact that her daughter was not feminine and demure and the pair argued constantly. Marie was much closer to her son, Mike, and like her parents before her never dished out discipline. Materially, the children wanted for nothing. Emotionally, it was a different story.

Going Up in the World

In 1962, Marie instigated a move to McClellan Boulevard, which was much closer to the houses of the affluent residents of Anniston that she so desperately tried to emulate. She felt that they were 'her' people. That same year, Marie's parents – Huey and Lucille moved in with the Hilleys.[7]

Marie's behaviour was becoming more and more out of control, and Frank was becoming increasingly concerned. He would often sit up with her during the night as she shook violently, unable to calm her. Perhaps the financial hole she had dug for the family was beginning to take its toll on Marie's psyche – by this time she had opened a Post Office Box and was having some of her bills sent there in order to avoid detection by Frank.

When the money ran out Marie started taking out loans. Frank was a well-respected man in the area and loans were secured against his good name and standing in the community. But creditors became concerned when bills and loan payment dates came and went without being settled, as Frank had always been a man who paid on time.[8]

On December 11th, 1965, Marie's father, Huey, died of cancer at the age of 57.[9]

In 1972, Mike graduated from High School and decided to pursue a career in the ministry, for which he went away to college.

Marie's behaviour towards her daughter, Carol, became more extreme. She often accused her of being a lesbian and would rant at Carol's female friends. Her paranoia at being found out in the lies regarding money must have been affecting her, because she also, around this time, stopped Frank from talking to his friends on the 'phone. It was also around this period of time that Frank Hilley became sick.[10]

Frank

During 1974 Frank had long periods of sickness. He put his frequent illnesses down to something he'd eaten, but soon the fatigue, vomiting and nausea could not be explained away by food. One day Frank came home from work early after succumbing to yet another bout of sickness, to find his wife in bed with her boss. His wife's spending suddenly made sense – she was sleeping with her employers for money. Frank was disgusted with his wife's behaviour but felt too ill and weak to deal with it. Instead, he turned to his son, Mike, who was by this time an ordained minister.[11]

However, that phone call, in which Frank arranged to meet Mike in Georgia where he now lived, was overheard by Audrey, who was listening in on an extension. From that moment on, Frank's symptoms worsened considerably, and he became seriously ill.[12]

On May 19th, 1975 Frank couldn't stand it any longer, and he consulted Dr Earl Jones, who diagnosed him initially with a viral stomach ache.[13] Dr Earl prescribed various medications, but nothing seemed to be helping. Frank's sister Freeda came to visit him, and he told her that he feared he was going to die, as he had never been so sick. He also told her that Marie had been administering him medicine via a syringe on the Dr's orders.[14]

On May 23rd, 1975, Frank was admitted to the Regional Medical Center. Tests indicated liver failure, and subsequently infectious hepatitis.[15] Frank was desperately ill, jaundiced and hallucinating. Mike, who had travelled to be with his father, had to restrain Frank from jumping out of the window. In the early hours of May 25th, Mike left the hospital to pick up his Grandmothers so that they could see Frank, but when he returned his mother was asleep and his father was dead. Frank Hilley was 45.[16]

Because of Frank's sudden death, an autopsy was performed, with Marie's blessing. Tests showed that Frank did indeed have hepatitis, along with swelling of the lungs and kidneys, inflammation of the stomach, and bilateral pneumonia.[17]

Life After Frank

With Frank's death being confirmed as being of natural causes, Marie made a claim on his life insurance and received a payment of $31,140.[18] Marie went on a spending spree, indulging her love of luxury items. She bought new clothes, jewelery, and a new car. Her mother, Lucille, was still living with Marie and Carol and received a diamond ring. Carol herself was treated to numerous gifts, including a car and a stereo. It was hardly the behaviour of a grieving widow.[19]

In 1976 Mike and his then wife Teri moved in with the family. Shortly after Frank's death, Lucille had been diagnosed with cancer. Her health was failing and they were happy to help. However, it wasn't a good move for the young couple. Marie was restless, and often complained to anyone who would listen that nobody loved her, and would frequently complain about her boss and her job. She was highly dissatisfied with her life, and to make matters worse Marie and Carol fought endlessly, making family life fraught. Mike would often find himself torn between his mother, who would constantly demand his attention, and his wife, Teri, who had begun experiencing ill health since moving in with Marie. Hospitalised four times with illness, Teri also suffered a miscarriage, and the young couple decided to move out.

They found an apartment and were ready to move in, but the night before their move Marie's house caught fire. Mike and Teri moved into their apartment, with Marie, Carol and Lucille in tow. Repairs were soon made to Marie's house, but the night before his mother was due to go home, Mike's neighbour's apartment suffered the same fate and went up in flames. Mike and Teri had no choice but to move back in with Marie, Carol and Lucille. They were back where they began.[20]

A Strange Series of Events

Mike and Teri finally found their own home and moved away from Marie. On January 4th, 1977, Lucille lost her battle against widespread, aggressive cancer. Marie again came into money – a small sum of $600 from a burial policy.

Marie became well known to the local police. She was constantly reporting strange occurrences at her home. As well as petty thefts, she claimed that a fire had been started in her closet late one night. Coincidentally, Marie's neighbour, Doris Ford reported an almost identical fire in her own house (to which Marie had a key) the same night. There followed a succession of reports by both women of nuisance phone calls and other grievances.

Marie came up with many theories about where the harassment of both herself and her neighbour was coming from. She told Detective Gary Caroll that she suspected someone at the phone company of making the calls, as the calls seemed only to happen when the trace was taken off of her phone. She also claimed that one of her former employers had tried to force her to have sex and was harassing her because of her refusal. Yet another theory put forward by Marie was that, shortly after Frank's death, two men had arrived at her house demanding repayment of gambling debts.

When police put a trace on Doris Ford's phone, however, the calls were traced back to the Jenkins Manufacturing Plant, which just so happened to be where Marie was working.[21]

In 1978, Marie and Carol moved to Florida to live with Mike and Teri. Carol had just graduated, and Marie found herself a job in an office. Her out of control spending habits continued to cause problems when she ran up over $600 on Mike's credit card, promising to pay him back. This living arrangement only lasted a few short months, however, before Marie and Carol returned to Anniston.[22]

Mike and Teri were happy to see Marie leave. By that time they had a baby son called Joshua, and Mike feared that Marie would take the baby and disappear as she seemed to have an unhealthy fixation on him.[23]

Carol's Turn

Marie had no home of her own to return to when she and Carol moved back to Anniston. At first, they stayed with Freeda, Frank's sister, and then they moved in with Carrie Hilley, Frank's mother. Once they were settled at Carrie's house, the strange happenings recommenced. Items went missing, phone lines were cut, and small fires were started. Illness also struck the household – Carrie Hilley started suffering from nausea and vomiting.

Marie started a new job, and very quickly started an affair with her boss, Harold Dillard, and began manipulating him to leave his wife. At the same time, she also started seeing Calvin Robertson, an old school friend. Calvin believed Marie when she told him she had cancer and needed expensive treatment, and he gladly gave her the money for the 'fictitious' illness. When Marie told him some time later that she was now cancer-free he was elated, and so smitten that he would have done anything for her.

It was also during this time that Marie began buying insurance policies. Not only did she take out fire insurance, cancer insurance, and her own life insurance, she also took out insurance policies on the lives of her two children. Mike was insured for $25,000 while Carol had two policies on her life, totalling $39,000.

Carol's senior prom came in April 1979. During the evening Carol started to feel ill. It wasn't enough to make her leave the party, though, so she ignored her symptoms. The next day, however, she was so ill during a church service that she had to leave the service early and vomited in the car park. Coincidentally, Carrie Hilley had also taken ill at church and was taken to hospital after fainting.[24]

By August 1979 Carol had been admitted to the Emergency Room several times with nausea and vomiting. After yet another episode of sickness in August, Marie gave her daughter an injection into her hip, which she said would ease the nausea. Instead of easing, however, Carol's illness took a serious downturn. Not only did the injection not ease Carol's sickness, it also caused her fingers and legs to become numb and weak.

On August 22nd, 1979 she was admitted to the Anniston Hospital by Dr Warren Sarrell. When, by August 29th Dr Sarrell had been unable to find a cause for Carol's symptoms, he sent her for a psychiatric evaluation at the Carraway Methodist Hospital in Birmingham. While under the care of Dr John Elmore, Carol was given two further injections by her mother – injections which, she was told, would help with her weak legs. She told Carol that the injections had been supplied by Doris Ford, who was a registered nurse, and that Carol could tell no-one as Doris would get into trouble if she was found out.

On September 18th, 1979, with Carol still in the hospital, Marie asked Dr Elmore what was wrong with her daughter. He told her that she was suffering from vitamin deficiencies and malnutrition, and, in his opinion, lead poisoning. Carol took exception to this diagnosis and, against Dr Elmore's advice, discharged Carol from the hospital.

On September 19th, Carol was once again admitted to the hospital, this time to the University of Alabama Hospital in Birmingham. The same day, Marie was arrested as her fraudulent ways finally caught up with her. Her arrest was what, ultimately, saved Carol's life. Marie was taken in for questioning, and Carol was examined by Dr Brian Thompson, who noticed that, along with the numbness in her hands and feet, Carol also had striations on her nails, called Aldridge Mee's Lines. He explained that these markings were typical of arsenic poisoning, and ordered tests on Carol's hair.

The initial findings revealed that Carol had over 50 times the normal arsenic level of human hair. Shockingly, when more detailed tests were carried out on October 3rd, 1979 they showed that the hair close to Carol's scalp had over 100 times the normal levels, while hair further down the hair shaft the levels were lower, right down to zero at the ends. This indicated, according to Forensic Scientist John Case, that Carol had been systematically poisoned with arsenic over a period of four to eight months, with the dosages given in increasingly higher strengths.

Furthermore, with Marie unable to be with her daughter, Carol's conditioned improved dramatically during her time at the hospital.[25]

On the strength of these findings, Frank Hilley's body was exhumed, and once again large levels of arsenic were found. His cause of death was changed to that of arsenic poisoning. The same substance was also discovered to have been present in both Lucille Frazier and Carrie Hilley (who had died recently) at the time of their deaths, although not fatal amounts.[26]

On October 9th, 1979, while still incarcerated for the fraudulent charges, Marie Hilley was arrested for the attempted murder of Carol. As part of their ongoing, and increasingly serious, investigations the Anniston police found a vial in Marie's purse – a vial which testing confirmed contained arsenic.

On November 9th, 1979, Marie made bail and was released, under the name of Emily Stephens, to a local motel. However, Marie was not going to just sit and await her trial, and somewhere between October 9th and October 18th, Marie disappeared. A note was found in her motel room, suggesting that she 'might' have been kidnapped.

Audrey Marie Hilley was now a fugitive and would remain so for more than three years.[27]

A New Identity

There were only a few clues for the police to go on after Marie disappeared. Margaret Key, Marie's Aunt, reported that her home had been broken into and that her car and some clothes had disappeared. The police called in the FBI, but once the car was found abandoned in Georgia the trail went cold very quickly.

On January 11th, 1980, Marie Hilley, still a fugitive, was indicted for the murder of her husband, Frank Hilley.

Marie, meanwhile, had assumed a new identity in Florida. Robbi Hannon, as she was now known, was working her charm on a man called John Homan. Robbi told John tales of her imaginary tragic past, and John, who hadn't had the easiest of lives himself, fell for both the stories and for Robbi. She told him that she had lost her children in a car accident and John felt as though he had found a kindred spirit.

He fell in love, hook, line, and sinker.

On May 29th, 1981 Robbi and John were married, after which they moved to Marlow, New Hampshire. They both found work there and rented a house. Robbi's new job was in customer service at the Central Screw Corporation, where she excelled. The men found her to be fun, while her co-workers, for the most part, found her pleasant, although a few took a dislike to her. She regaled the staff with stories of a wealthy family in Texas, whose fortune she would inherit one day, and garnered sympathy by telling them about her two children dying in a car accident.

She would also talk of an identical twin sister called Teri Martin, who lived in Texas, making frequent reference to her.

Robbi would, from time to time, complain of searing headaches, and told John that she was seeking treatment from specialists. Until one day, Robbi came to John and told him it had been discovered that she was suffering from an incurable blood disease. It was her twin sister, Teri, who would be looking after Robbi when she made one last trip to Texas in search of a cure, and in September 1982, Robbi left Marlow to seek treatment.

Of course, there was no incurable disease, and no twin sister, either. Robbi only stayed in Texas for a few days, and then made her way to Florida, where she bleached her hair blond, and found work as a secretary, using the name Teri Martin. During her six weeks at her new job, Teri confided in her boss, Jack McKenzie, about her terminally ill twin sister Robbie. In early November, Teri called Jack and told him Robbi had died, and that she was needed in New Hampshire.

On November 10th, 'Teri' called John Homan and told him his wife had died, and the following day she flew back to New Hampshire.

During her time away, 'Teri' had lost a lot of weight, and changed her hair color to blond, so John easily accepted that this was his dead wife's twin sister. The pair went to the local paper and placed an obituary for Robbi, and then John took Teri to his wife's workplace – The Central Screw Corporation – and introduced the workers to Robbi's twin sister. While some of the staff accepted Teri's appearance, some did not and were highly suspicious.

Teri insisted on moving in with John Homan, saying they needed to help each other grieve, and she found herself a job as a secretary at a book printing company.

Meanwhile, the suspicions were still rising at Robbi's old workplace, and a few of the doubters decided to take a closer look into Robbi's obituary. Their suspicions were confirmed when they discovered that the details mentioned in the paper were fictitious, and they took those suspicions to the police.

Arrested

On January 12th, 1983, the police apprehended Teri at work. They had been watching her and thought she might be another fugitive, Terry Lynn Clifton. However, when they asked her her name she told them it was Audrey Marie Hilley, and that she was wanted for fraud. The local police ran a check on her name and discovered that she was wanted for much more than bad checks.

On January 19th, 1983, Marie was brought back to Anniston. Carol was desperate to see her mother, to find some answers, but although Marie professed her love for her daughter she gave no explanation for the poisoning. Prosecutors were worried that Carol's love for her mother would go in Marie's favour and that Carol would not say anything against her mother.

They needn't have worried.

Carol's testimony about her mother giving her the injections was solid. Marie had told her attorneys that after her arrest in 1979 she had been interviewed but she failed to mention that that interview had been recorded. During that interview, Marie admitted to giving Carol the injections and the recording was there for all to hear. Carol's defense fell apart.

The jury needed only three hours to return their verdicts – guilty of the murder of Frank Hilley, and of the attempted murder of Carol Hilley.

Judge Sam Monk sentenced Marie to life imprisonment for Frank's murder, plus twenty years for the poisonings, and on June 9th, 1983, Marie was taken to Tutwiler State Women's Prison in Wetumpka, Alabama.

Marie's Escape

Marie was a perfect prisoner. She never caused trouble and was classified as a minimum security prisoner. This classification meant that she was eligible for leave from the prison. Between late 1986 and February 1987, Marie had left prison for eight hours on four occasions, returning on time with each leave.

On February 19th, 1987, Marie left the prison on a three-day leave pass. John had, by this time, moved to Anniston so that he and his wife could spend her leave together whenever they could.

On February 22nd, Marie arranged to meet John at her parents' graves. Marie never showed up, and John found, instead, a note from his wife.

"I hope you will be able to forgive me," it read. *"I'm getting ready to leave. It will be best for everybody. We'll be together again. Please give me an hour to get out of town."*

John took the note to the police, and, given Marie's past cunning, they assumed she was already far out of state, and started, once again, searching for her.[28]

Her Death

Marie hadn't gone far. On February 26th, 1987, Aniston police received a phone call. Marie had been found huddled behind a house, apparently having wandered in the woods for four days. The weather had been terrible – heavy rain and low temperatures – and Marie was suffering from hypothermia and delirium. Marie started having convulsions, and, in the ambulance on the way to the hospital, Audrey Marie Hilley took her last breath.

On February 28th, 1987, Marie was buried next to her husband, Frank, at their children's request.[29] Her second husband, John Homan, died two years later in 1989 while working as a caretaker in Anniston. He intervened in a fight and was stabbed to death. Marie's note to John, in which she said that they would be together again, had come true a lot sooner than anyone would have predicted.[30]

HOUSEWIFE, MOTHER & KILLER : THE TRUE STORY OF KIM HRICKO

62

DARLA PUGH

PROLOGUE

Kim Hricko was getting ready to kill her husband the night they attended a Valentine's Murder Mystery Party. Kim was a woman who was intelligent and determined, the irony of the play's theme was not lost on her.

It was destiny calling.

She watched with rapt attention as the actors went through the motions. A wedding bride took out a blue vial and poured the "poisonous" contents into her groom's champagne glass.

She has the right idea, Kim thought.

Looking over at her husband Steve, she imagined him in the place of the actor on stage, choking to death.

Could it be that easy?

CHAPTER ONE

"Kim Hricko was one of those people that you look at and say 'I would never have guessed,'" forensic psychologist Paula Orange said. "Something inside her snapped when she wanted out of her marriage. It could have been so simple. Call a lawyer and file for divorce. Kim wanted a lot more than that. She wanted blood."

Steve and Kim Hricko would be introduced by their mutual friends Maureen and Mike Miller at Penn State in 1984. Their temperaments seemed to be the perfect complement to one another, they would have a yin-yang compatibility.

"Kim was a very gregarious personality," Maureen said. "She was very outgoing. Very friendly. Everybody liked her."

"Steve was my best friend since seventh grade," Mike said. "Corny as it sounds we were kinda each others brother that we didn't have. My wife had set up a double date. He (Steve) was smitten by her. Thought she was very attractive. Basically, they hit it off and from that point on started dating."

Steve was a burly figure at 6'3" and 245 lbs. He was a star college football player but was on the shy side.

"He was a big teddy bear," Maureen said. "He just wanted everybody that he loved to be happy and for him to take care of them."

Neither Kim or Steve dated much before their union. Kim had a distant relationship with her father after her own parents divorced. Her mother would remarry a man that would sexually and physically abuse her.

Steve and Kim would marry and have a daughter. Nine years into their marriage, Steve would still be smitten by the woman that the Millers had set him up with. Kim, however, would have feelings of resentment that built up over time.

Temperamentally, the couple did not match up well. Steve was an introvert. Kim an extrovert. Kim hung out with doctors and nurses while Steve just wanted to stay home. He didn't feel welcome into Kim's elite social circle, put off by their large houses and flashy cars.

But Steve remained in love with Kim despite that over the years she did not treat him with the same warmth as she once did. She was now cold and disinterested toward her spouse.

Steve blamed himself for the deterioration and began working to save his marriage.

His efforts would only serve to pour fuel on the fire...

CHAPTER TWO

Kim fed up with the loveless relationship, suggested that they get a divorce but Steve refused. He also dismissed the idea of counseling but after nine years he finally saw it as a last resort.

Steve went to counseling on his own and began taking steps to show Kim how much he truly cared. One of the first things he did was write his wife a long, heartfelt love letter.

Kim shared the letter with some of her friends who remarked at how beautiful it was. But Steve's words of love and devotion had no effect on Kim.

"Can you believe this shit?" Kim mocked as she read some passages aloud. "I am willing to do whatever it takes to save our marriage. It takes two of us. But I know we can do it. Together."

"I think that's sweet," her friend remarked.

"Gag me," Kim rolled her eyes. "Trust me, when you've been married as long as I have this kind of syrupy shit only makes you sick."

"I wish my husband would write me love letters."

"No," Kim said. "You don't. They keep coming and they don't stop. He's smothering me and following me around the house like a puppy dog."

Steve's renewed efforts to rekindle a long dead marriage were now being met with resentment. He was earnest in displaying his affection and becoming more communicative with Kim.

"Let's talk about our feelings," he said to his wife who stiffened with his every touch.

Kim would go to work eager to vent. She would open up about her marital difficulties to anyone who was willing to listen. She found a confidante in Jennifer Gowen.

"He is suffocating me," Kim told Gowen. "Stifling me. Following me around the damn house the whole time and cuddling with me at night. I can't even breathe. He's always asking me where I'm going or what I'm doing. Now he's calling me on my cell just to say 'Hi'. He never used to do that. It is annoying as shit."

But Steve was merely following the advise of his counsel. He had not dated much before Kim and she was his first serious relationship. He had no idea what to do when the relationship turned sour.

"It has to be said that Steve was on the receiving end of some very bad counseling advice," Orange said. "Appeasement never works and that is something that any decent psychiatrist or counselor should know. He kept turning the other cheek with Kim and that just fueled her resentment of him even more. This isn't to justify his murder, of course."

With his counseling session inspired efforts not yielding any results, Steve became distraught. He had done everything by the book but it wasn't working. He called his close friend Mike and opened up about his marriage and job difficulties.

"I don't know what to do, man," Steve said, his voice quaking with emotion. "I don't want to lose her. She's my life. My family is my everything. I feel like I've already lost her."

"Take it easy," Mike said. "We'll figure something out."

"What do you think I should do?" Steve asked.

"You need to take her out," Mike said "Someplace special. You know. Make a memory."

"Yeah," Steve said. "I know that. But I'm at a loss at how to go about it. I've tried everything."

"Tell you what," Mike said. "You come over to the Golf Resort."

"Harbourtowne?"

"I'll make sure you get the honeymoon cottage we have here. The very best one."

"You're too cool, Mike."

"Anytime, brother."

Mike worked at the Harbourtowne Golf Resort and set up the accommodations for his good friend and his wife. The place was hosting a Valentine's Day Murder Mystery play. Mike knew that the place worked wonders for romance. If there was anyplace that could rekindle the spark in a relationship, the resort would be it.

But Steve didn't know that Kim already had a romance of her own. His name was Brad Winkler.

CHAPTER THREE

Kim had met Brad Winkler when she was planning out the bachelorette party for her co-worker, Jennifer Gowen. Jennifer had brought Brad to the wedding shower ahead of time and the United States Marine was the only man at the party aside from Steve.

Kim and the young man hit it off immediately. She gave him a ride home along with Norma Walz after the party was over. They dropped off Brad at his aunt's house and Kim watched from the car as the young man made his way inside.

"He was in a bad marriage," Kim said to Norma. "Pretty sad. He's a nice guy. Jesus. The girl who catches him is going to be a lucky one. He's really sweet."

Kim returned home and was chastised by Steve for spending so much time with Brad. He had no idea of the affair to come.

Jennifer Gowen would get married and enlist the aid of Brad to help around the house while she was away on her honeymoon. Jennifer had a one-year-old daughter and Brad would babysit the girl and do some chores around the place.

Kim would come over and help out with the baby on the day Gowen left.

The affair with Brad would begin that night. They would have their trysts at Jen's townhouse while his cousin was still on her honeymoon. When Jennifer returned, the couple would continue their affair at the home of Brad's aunt.

Kim was equally open about her affair with Brad Winkler among friends as she was about her dissatisfaction with her marriage.

"I'm seeing someone," Kim said to Rachel, her college friend.

"You're having an affair?"

"Its just sex," Kim said, shrugging her shoulder. "I'm not going to marry this guy."

Kim kept up the charade on the home front as she plotted her next move. The change in her behavior made Steve believe that his efforts were working as he chronicled in his journal.

"Life at home is improving," Steve wrote. "I am looking forward to Valentine's weekend at Harbourtowne with Kim. She called twice today and said 'I love you' without me saying it first. I was very happy. Kim and I have not made love yet and I want to but I will wait as long as it takes. I love her...I believe I know what being in love really is. We have been married nine years but I feel like we just started dating."

Sadly, four days after Steve wrote those words in his journal Kim was off buying Brad Winkler a Valentine's Day gift.

"Brad, I really want to give you all these gifts in person but I guess the Pentagon had a different idea," Kim wrote. "I am so proud of what you do so I'll just go on missing you. Have a nice weekend at home, baby. I look forward to seeing you soon. Happy Valentine's Day, sir. I love you so very much. Hugs and Kisses, Kim."

While Steve had an optimistic view of their future life together, Kim continued to tell anyone with a listening ear about her dissatisfaction.

"There is a lot of verbal abuse," Kim said to Theresa Armstrong, one of her neighbors. "From both of us. He doesn't do anything. I do everything. I am unhappy and don't want to be married to him anymore."

She then went to her job at Holy Cross Hospital and told her co-worker Norma Walz about her problems.

"I've been in a bad marriage for a long time," Kim said. "Me and Steve have been having problems for a long time. A very long time."

"I always suspected that something wasn't right," Norma said.

"I've been living a lie," Kim nodded. I wanted him to go to counseling two years ago. Now he's going. And he's driving me crazy."

Steve's constant fawning and pandering annoyed Kim so much that she began thinking about what life would be like without him.

"You know if my husband dies we'd be better off than if we got a divorce," Kim told one of her neighbors. "Steve doesn't make that much money. He's a groundskeeper. We get a divorce and I'm paying him alimony. But if he died, well, if he died we would inherit $450,000 from his life insurance."

"That's a morbid thing to think about," the neighbor said, trying to laugh it off.

"You read about these stories all the time. The husband killing off the wife and vice-versa. I always wondered why they did it instead of just getting a divorce. It's the life insurance. Just like in the movies."

"What was lost in Kim's rationalizing was the fact that the killers most always get caught," Orange said. "But in her mind, she was the special one. Narcissists always think like that. Like they are the special one that won't get caught. Still, Kim needed that reassurance from her peers that she was doing the right thing as crazy as it sounds."

After not getting a receptive response from her neighbor, Kim once again turned to Jennifer Gowen.

"Steve would be better off dead," Kim said, using the same line on Jennifer. "We talked about getting a divorce but Steve doesn't want that. Even if he did he is going to try and turn Anna against me or try to keep her. He doesn't have a life outside our marriage so he is better off dead anyway."

"You really shouldn't talk like that. Let alone think like that."

"Why not? I thought about telling him about Brad but I think he would just get depressed or suicidal. Then I would not be able to collect the insurance if he killed himself."

"You think he'd kill himself?"

"Probably," Kim said. "So I have to figure something else out. You know there was this serial killer. I forgot her name. But she would go around in the children's ward and shoot the kids up with Succinylcholine. It is a muscle paralyzer. No way to trace it."

Kim would later inform Gowen that if she could kill Steve and get away with it that she "would do it tomorrow."

Seeking other alternatives aside from poisoning, Kim approached fellow surgical tech Ken Burges in the locker room of the hospital.

"Hi, Ken."

"Hey there," Ken said.

"Do you know of anyone that could kill my husband?"

"What?" Ken asked. He thought Kim was playing a joke.

"Do you know anyone that can, you know, kill someone? For a price."

"I'm insulted that you would ask me that. Do I look that sketchy to you?"

Burges had been convicted of welfare fraud in Virginia a couple of years before obtaining his job at the hospital. Because of this, Kim may have presumed that he would be the type of person who would know people capable of such an act.

"I got $50,000 for anyone who could do something like that."

"You got the wrong dude," Ken said. "The wrong guy."

"Forget I even asked," Kim said.

"You work in the operating room," Ken advised. "You could just put him to sleep."

Ken didn't know that Kim already had that idea in mind.

Kim began to plot out details of the murder. She needed to do something that was untraceable. This called for poison. She had to burn away any evidence so her attack had to take place away from home.

She ran her plan by a college friend of hers, Rachel McCoy. Kim justified her actions by demonizing her husband. She talked about his unwillingness to do stuff with her as he was a homebody and kept a messy home. Their personalities were too different.

Then without warning, she began articulating her plan to kill Steve with the poison and then setting the place on fire.

It was almost as if she wanted Rachel to poke any holes in her plan should she miss anything.

Rachel tried to talk Kim out of the hare-brained idea to no avail. She suggested simply getting a divorce but Kim was convinced that killing Steve was "easier." Rachel also brought up the fact that she was robbing their daughter, Anna, of a father.

"She would be better off without him," Kim said.

Whatever Rachel suggested, Kim had an answer for.

Her mind was made up.

Steve had to go.

CHAPTER FOUR

Kim knew that the drug she had to obtain was Succinylcholine. It would be readily available to her as she did her rounds through the hospital. Just walk by a tray of meds in the surgery unit and lift one of the vials. Easy peasy.

"I'm going to get this drug," Kim told her friend Rachel. "It will paralyze Steve. Stop his breathing and then I'll set the curtains on fire with a candle or a cigar. He won't be able to move and then he'll die of smoke inhalation. Nobody will know shit."

Kim would not take into account the fact that her husband was a healthy and robust man with no medical history. That would certainly draw suspicion.

"This would be the only logical explanation for what brought about Steven Hricko's death," prosecuting attorney Robert Dean said.

"Because there was nothing else wrong with him. His body organs were in fine shape, there was no trauma. It had to have been this. She had to have carried through her plan."

"Kim was determined," Orange said. "She wanted her cake and eat it too. It is a head scratcher as to why she didn't pursue a divorce but the mind of a sociopath works differently. She wanted a clean break. If she had gotten a divorce, then Steve would have remained in her life forever the next ten years because of their daughter. She wanted to erase him from the picture and nothing and nobody was going to talk her out of it."

The planned romantic getaway loomed on the horizon for Valentine's Day weekend. Steve looked forward to their alone time together with giddy excitement. He told his counselor that this would be the turning point where the sparks of romance would once again be rekindled.

But Kim looked toward the weekend with dread. She had told Jennifer Gowen that she had only had sex with Steve once in the past six months and the experience left her feeling repulsed.

"I'm not looking forward to the trip," Kim said in her own counseling session.

"Why?" her counselor asked. "It may be an opportunity to rekindle some passion."

"I'm tired and really don't feel up to the trip. It's a long drive. It is going to be miserable."

Then a light bulb flashed in Kim's mind. The resort would be the perfect place.

The perfect place to put her plans into effect.

CHAPTER SIX

Valentine's Day weekend arrived.

Steve had romance on his mind. His forehead perspired as he felt the anxiety of trying to save his marriage.

Kim had Brad Winkler on her mind as she looked out the car window.

Then her mind drifted to murder.

She had to set everything up just right. Inject Steve. Burn the cottage room. Then tell the police her story and stick with it no matter what.

Kim and Steve drove from their home in Laurel, Maryland to St Michaels. It would be a 75-mile to a romantic getaway that many had christened as the "Heart & Soul of Chesapeake Bay."

But the couple arrived at their cottage and found the place to be freezing. Kim started a fire in the wood stove then made some coffee.

The conversation was muted and awkward. They decided to watch some TV before looking out the window and taking in the view of the bay. It was windy and the the cold, damp weather chased them back inside

Preparing for the dinner, Steve popped a few Effexor tablets for his depression which had gotten worse in recent weeks. He also took an anti-anxiety medication called Xanax and a muscle relaxant called Flexeril.

Getting dressed, they attended the interactive murder mystery dinner called THE BRIDE WHO CRIED. The actors staged a re-enactment of a woman killing her soon to be husband. The actors encouraged audience members to ask the actors questions in an attempt to find out who the murderer was.

Kim enjoyed the play immensely. When the actors called for audience participation, she was one of two women who went out onto the stage and began asking questions like a detective.

The play now over, Kim and Steve returned to their cottage. Not yet having their fill of entertainment, the couple would watch the comedy film "Tommy Boy". They got a good laugh out of it but according to Kim they "still did not talk about our problems."

Steve then fell asleep.

Kim stood over him like a predator then went to the bathroom to prepare her lethal cocktail of succinylcholine. Building up her nerve, she finally did the move that she had been practicing in her head for two years.

Kim pulled aside the bed sheet and injected the syringe into his neck.

I'll burn the body. That will get rid of the puncture wound.

Kim also knew that the drug she administered only caused paralysis. It didn't affect a patient's level of consciousness.

So when Kim set the room on fire, Steve would know that he was being burned to death.

And he wouldn't be able to do anything about it.

The thought made Kim smile. She didn't want to just kill him. She wanted to make him suffer. To humiliate him.

Kim pulled the now paralyzed but awake Steve off the bed and dropped him to the floor. She doused his body with lighter fluid.

Kim, what are you doing? Steve looked up at his wife, unable to move or speak.

"Call it the perfect crime," she whispered in his ear as if reading his thoughts.

He stared straight up at the ceiling, catching Kim's movements in the corner of his eye.

He heard a matchstick strike against a box.

Then he felt a sharp pain race up his body as she set him ablaze.

I can't move, Steven thought as terror and pain engulfed him.

I can't breathe.

I can't breathe.

Kim, what are you doing?

I brought you here to save our marriage. I have done what I could do making this better.

I love you. Please don't do this!

Kim poured more of the lighter fluid onto Steve's body. She lit another match and threw it on him.

"She injected him with succinylcholine and watched him suffocate," Maureen said. "And lit him on fire. How much colder could it get."

CHAPTER FIVE

Kim Hricko walked into the resort reception area with a calm demeanor. She had her ear to her cell phone which was turned upside down.

"I need to talk to someone who works here," she informed desk clerk Elaine Phillips.

"I work here," Elaine said, expecting Kim's response being anything from wanting more towels to complaining about faulty air conditioning.

"My room is on fire."

"Is there anyone else in the room?" Phillips asked.

"Yeah," she said without emotion. "My husband."

"What room are you in?" Elaine asked, making her way around the corner of the desk.

Elaine and another hotel employee hurried into the courtyard of the resort.

"You smell that?" Elaine asked. "Something is definitely burning."

The two sprinted to cottage number 506 at the end of the resort. The door was shut but there was a tiny opening in the sliding door in the rear.

Smoke filled the room. They could barely see one foot in front of them. Kneeling down, one of the employees saw the the prone figure of a man inside. He crawled in, braving the smoke and pulled the body to safety on the back porch.

It was too late.

Steve Hricko, burned to a crisp.

The man had died with a Playboy magazine at his side with his pajama pants down at his knees as if he collapsed while masturbating.

"I want to see his dead body," Kim said as she milled around with the hotel guests watching the scene.

"I thought it was odd," one of the guests said. "Because no one had pronounced anyone to be dead yet."

Kim gave her statement to the Sheriff then called their best friends, Mike and Maureen Miller.

"It's the last thing you expect when you receive a phone call at night," Maureen said. "When the phone rings at night you know that it's not anything good."

"My wife answered the phone," Mike Miller said. "And sort of roused me a little bit and said that there's was an incident in Steve and Kim's room. Kim's requesting that you come down there as soon as possible.

The Millers were shocked at the sudden death of Steve. They were even more shocked at the demeanor of Kim when they went to console her.

"I didn't expect her to be anything less than a hysterical woman whose husband passed away," Maureen said. "She was the exact opposite. Just exact opposite."

Kim told everyone that Steve was drunk and made advances toward her. He groped and fondled her but she didn't want to have sex. They argued and she left the cottage.

Mike knew that something was fishy. His friend Steve was not a drinker.

Did Kim plan this out?

"They said the fire started because of him carelessly smoking," Mike said. "Steve doesn't smoke. All the years I've known Steve, I've never seen him smoke a cigarette, a cigar. He despised being around people that smoked."

An autopsy was performed and forensic pathologist Janis Amatuzio, like Mike Miller, quickly realized that something was amiss.

"Steven's body was found in a fire," Amatuzio said. "The major question for the forensic pathologist is that did he die of the fire or not. When there was no soot in the airways, when there was no damage to the lungs. It suggested that Steven was dead before the fire started."

"Steven was not drunk that night," prosecuting attorney Robert Dean said. "The drug tests and the autopsy shows that. Steve was not drunk."

The picture didn't fit. Steve was not a drinker nor was he a smoker. But friends and family could not believe the worst about Kim Hricko. The fun and outgoing mother could not have killed her own husband, the man who adored her for the past nine years.

Could she?

"Was she really capable of doing this?" Maureen asked. "Everybody was saying it but again, I ignored it and just pushed it back and said that she wasn't capable of doing it. Man, was I wrong."

CHAPTER SIX

Police began their investigation and discovered that Kim left a trail of incriminating conversations as well as evidence.

"Kim was too smart for her own good," Orange said. "She did her research on succinylcholine, did her research on the how quickly a body burns. But she did not know how to stage a killing."

Kim had left empty beer bottles in the room and a pack of cigars. The cigars would be the clue that blew Kim's story up in smoke.

Steve was not a smoker and the cigars she had left behind as evidence were not the kind to start a fire.

"There was an investigation as to how a fire like this could have started," prosecuting attorney Robert Dean said. "That fire could not have started by the ashes of a cigar."

Kim would state that after she and Steve had gotten into a fight she went for a drive. She wanted to visit Mike and Maureen Miller who only lived minutes away. She stated she had become lost. The prosecution thought that her excuse seemed odd as she had visited the Millers on numerous occasions. She also had a brother who lived only a few blocks away from the Miller home. And why had she not simply called them on her cell phone?

"I didn't want to wake anyone," Kim said when asked why she didn't call.

Her answer was incongruent as why would she worry about waking someone up with a cell phone call when she didn't have a problem arriving on their doorstep in the middle of the night?

Nine days after the murder, police would arrive at the home of a Hricko friend where Kim had been staying. They had a search warrant for her car but Kim felt the noose tightening around her neck. She ran to the bathroom room and locked it behind herself as the police entered the home.

Kim then swallowed a whole bottle of Xanax.

"Come out of there, Kim," the police yelled.

They busted the door down and saw Kim there in the bathtub, holding a razor blade over her wrist.

"I'll kill myself!" she screamed. "I'll fucking do it!"

The officers quickly subdued Kim without further incident. They then transported her to a psychiatric facility where she was put on suicide watch.

The trial would only last six days as the prosecuting attorney detailed how Kim staged the murder.

"She stated that he was sloppy drunk," prosecuting attorney Robert Dean said. "And that he wanted to have sex. She said they got into an argument and that she left for a few hours. She said she drove around and got lost. And then she returned to the cottage and saw that it was full of smoke and then she reported that the room was on fire."

The case against Kim was made by several friends, co-workers, and neighbors. They all testified about the affair, the plot to kill Steve and her desire to acquire the drug succinylcholine.

Kim Hricko would be found guilty of murder and arson. She would be sentenced to life in prison.

"It's sad that he (Steve) is not the one in the world anymore and she is," Maureen said.

"He was my best friend," Mike said. "And the fact that he isn't here anymore is pretty hard for me to take."

The other victim aside from Steve was their nine-year-old daughter. She lost both her father and her mother.

"Her child is the victim," Maureen said. "And is forever going to wonder which side of the family is telling the truth. Is it true that her mother was unjustly accused or is it true that she's a cold, manipulating, calculating murderer."

END

KILLER CHURCH LADY : THE TRUE STORY OF BLANCHE MOORE

KATIE STONE

"People couldn't believe that she did what she did. People became fascinated that how could someone who on the surface could be so nice, could be capable of such a heinous crime." - Paula Orange

Blanche Taylor Moore was born on February 17th, 1933 in North Carolina, the fifth of seven children. Her father was Parker Davis Kiser, a self-taught minister who had both a drinking and gambling problem. Her mother, Flonnie Honeycutt, held little sway in the goings on in the Kiser household. Flonnie would work in the local mills, bringing home $40 a week. She turned the money over to her husband who promptly turned around and spent the money on younger women. Kiser did various odd jobs to support the family, primarily working in a saw mill then later as an insurance salesman. His primary occupation, however, was the seduction of women that he came across in both bars and churches.

The Reverend Kiser was a strict father and didn't allow any of his children to participate in school activities or spend hanging out with friends.

Living a double life, P.D. Kiser's gambling debts increased to the point where he made the decision to sell young Blanche off as a prostitute to pay off his debts which he incurred during card games.

After one losing streak, Reverend Kiser took his adolescent daughter for a drive and pulled over to the side of the road.

"I'm going to pull up under that tree," Kiser said. "When I do, I want you to go fuck that man."

"P.D. Kiser was an alcoholic and self-righteous country minister," said psychologist Kelleher. "Despite efforts to abstain from alcohol he always relapsed. Blanche's childhood was utterly destroyed by her father and she lived in a childhood prison of despair."

Blanche, desperate to leave the abusive household, married James Taylor in May of 1952. Blanche was nineteen years old at the time,

Taylor was twenty-four. She would give birth to their first daughter, Vanessa, in 1953.

Blanche was the typical Southern diva, confident in her ability to seduce any man she wanted but found the pickings slim in her small North Carolina town. She was attractive by most accounts, having long black hair and eyes that "were so dark they looked black."

"Blanche's face was sculpted in the high bird-boned features of the very prettiest Appalachian women," one researcher said. "Long, lithe, with generous breasts and a sleek round bottom perched on slender, perfectly shaped legs."

"She flew her small burgh of Tarheel by grabbing the first man who asked her to marry him. Young Blanche was left with one overwhelming wish for the future-to leave her perverse, sermonizing father and begin a new life that was far away from his abuse."

Finances were tough and Blanche was forced to work as a cashier at the Kroger supermarket. She would toil on the job for six years before giving birth to their second child, Cindi, in 1953. Still, she became a popular fixture at the market as folks would line up at her register just to have a quick chat with the friendly Blanche. She would remain a mainstay at the supermarket for decades.

"She was always friendly to customers and her co-workers," a former Kroger employee said. "You would have never guessed her as being unhappy or mean to anyone. Just wasn't in her."

Her tenure at Kroger's looked to be mixed, however, as Blanche could be moody. But the management hierarchy gave her high marks in her job performance and labeled her as a "good leader" as she trained other grocery checkers.

Still, a dark side emerged.

"She could be vindictive," said one co-worker who asked not to be identified. "If you got on her bad side, watch out. She was two-faced. Two-faced and underhanded. There was one incident where a large bag of cash wound up missing. Management would have to explain why her store was the only store that didn't turn a profit."

BAD MARRIAGE

By 1959, things had soured at the homefront. Blanche and James had several loud fights in public. Blanche was dragged behind a car on one occasion and in another she was confronted about an affair with a customer at the Kroger supermarket.

Despite her peculiar manner, Blanche would be promoted to "head cashier" which was the equivalent of a store manager in today's corporate climate. This was one of the few top positions open to Kroger's women employees at that time. She would also sell Tupperware at home parties which she used as a cover to seduce different men that interested her.

Her husband James seemed powerless against the woman he married. He worked as a furniture restorer but jobs were few and far between for the former military veteran who had just returned from the Korean War. James was described as a "burly man" that was "quick to anger." He spent the majority of his time editing sermons taken from the Glen Hope Baptist church and sending them overseas for missionaries to spread the gospel. He also began drowning himself in alcohol which was much to Blanche's disappointment.

"Blanche had, in essence, married a carbon copy of her father," forensic psychologist Paula Orange said. "James was like her dad in that he was a compulsive gambler and was horrible with money. He would disappear on the weekend and come back flat broke."

Her own father wouldn't behave much better, leaving Blanche's mother in 1960 as he vowed to "find himself a younger woman."

Blanche then acted out on her own. She continued to use the supermarket as her own personal singles bar, having affairs with numerous customers and male supervisors.

James would find out about her affairs and would threaten to leave Blanche. The two would continue to have violent, explosive arguments but ultimately James would never follow through on his threats to leave.

A NEW MAN

By 1962, however, Blanche would have her sights set on a new assistant manager by the name of Raymond Reid.

Reid was already married with two young children and initially spurned the advances of the slightly older Blanche.

But what Blanche wanted, Blanche got. It took three years of flirting to finally get Raymond to lower his guard. Blanche seduced the married man but continued to sleep with other male companions she met through the store.

To further complicate her life, Blanche's father had taken ill shortly after she arrived to make some sort of attempt at reconciliation.

Blanche remained at his bedside and helped to try and nurse him back to health. The elder Kiser, however, was too far gone. He died due to "heart attack triggered by chronic emphysema."

Doctors completely overlooked the fact that Kiser had suffered from violent stomach cramps, diarrhea, vomiting, delirium and a blue skin pallor.

This all pointed to death by arsenic poisoning but they had no reason to suspect Blanche of anything.

Noting the ease with she got away with her father's death, Blanche set her sights on the other man who was an obstacle to her happiness.

Her husband, James Taylor would suffer a near-fatal heart attack. His brush with death forced him to "get right with God" and he attempted to reconcile with Blanche.

"James Taylor's life trajectory was strikingly similar to that of Blanche's father, Parker Davis," Orange said. "Like Davis, he would find religion later in life and put on the pretense of a changed man. Blanche saw through it all, she herself was used to men using religion as a prop much like her father. But she put up appearances for appearance sake."

Blanche would later describe James as becoming "the perfect husband and father" but her six-year affair with Raymond Reid continued.

Despite their marital infidelity, Blanche would try and persuade Reid to attend church with her.

"I have been quite religious all my life, or I was," Blanche recalled. "I was very active in the First Disciples until the fire. After that, I just lost my interest in religion."

With his wife deeply entrenched in an affair, James would come down with the "flu" in September of 1970. He started to lose his hair, had diarrhea, swollen glands, blood stool and blue skin pallor. All the signs of arsenic poisoning yet no one who examined him was any the wiser. He would be hospitalized at the end of the month and die a few dies after his admission, shortly after Blanche brought him some ice cream.

Blanche would then help take care of James' mother, Isla, up until her death on November 25th, 1970. Doctors signed off on Isla's death as something attributed to natural causes. Inexplicably, they ignored the blue skin pallor on the woman as well as the undigested arsenic that remained in the Blanche's mother-in-law's stomach.

So within two months, Blanche had eliminated both her husband James and her mother-in-law, Isla. She was able to obtain a small portion of their estate and used the money to buy a home in Burlington, North Carolina.

Despite proceeds from these deaths, her co-workers thought she may have been "tapping the till" at work as there was no way she could afford such a home on the meager inheritance.

COAST IS CLEAR

Raymond Reid would decide to go all in on his affair with Blanche. He left his wife and children in 1971, a full nine years after first meeting Blanche. He got himself a small apartment and filed for divorce from his wife, fully expecting Blanche to become his bride.

Blanche would stop by at Reid's new place, cook him breakfast and sexually entertain him. She said that Reid was "helpless" without her.

This caused a stir not only in their workplace but in the small town in which they both lived.

"Mom never expected to spend the rest of her life by herself. She had too much to offer," said Blanche's daughter Cynthia Chatman.

"Reid was a very good man. He was good to us," said Vanessa, Blanche's other daughter.

Blanche herself didn't feel that way. As a future district attorney said while investigating Blanche's story, she would soon deem the young Reid as someone who "wasn't good enough, she wanted to date someone better. She was very blunt about that."

Blanche had a foul mouth and often said things that were inappropriate. Once she told the friend of her son-in-law, "you know what you really need? You need a really good blow job. If I went down on you, it'd probably kill you. You probably couldn't handle it."

She wouldn't limit her romantic encounters with the male supervisors like Reid at the supermarket. She targeted anyone she found handsome as when a new delivery man entered the store, Blanche said, "Man, I'd like to see the dick on that guy."

SEXUAL HARASSMENT

The highly sexual Blanche would claim sexual harassment during her tenure at Kroger's. A top company official named Robert J. Hutton paid a visit to her store. Blanche would contend that he made advances and fondled female cashiers.

"He reached him up my dress, exposed himself and grabbed my buttocks," Blanche said as she recalled an encounter with Hutton. "He had his pants down and asked 'Are you ready for this?'"

Blanche then picked up Hutton's pants and underwear as she fled from the store. EmbaRrassed, Hutton had to borrow a meat cutter's smock before exiting the store.

Blanche didn't return to Kroger's after the incident. She filed a sexual harassment suit and began seeing psychiatrists. One of her doctors, Dr. Jesse N. McNeil said in an affidavit that Blanche suffered from "depression, anxiety, and a serious suicidal condition. She felt completely alienated and antagonistic toward men and has not been able to maintain any meaningful social contacts with members of the opposite sex.

Her defense attorney would later dismiss the affidavit as "hyperbole" to bolster the charges of the sexual harassment suit.

It would later be revealed that Blanche had a flirtatious relationship with Hutton before she filed suit. She was on the lookout for someone "better" than Reid and thought that Hutton may fit the bill. But the relationship soured and Hutton ultimately lost his job.

Kroger would settle out of court with Blanche, paying the flirtatious young cashier a lump-sum payment of $275,000.

YET ANOTHER RUSE

Always on the look out for "quick cash," Blanche concocted a scheme to collect some fire insurance in 1985. A mysterious fire broke out at her home and Blanche put the blame on a local "pervert", a man that she claimed to have seen lurking around her property.

"I saw a man," Blanche said. "He was creeping around the side wall."

"Did you call the cops?"

"No," Blanche said. "He was, you know, touching himself. Touching himself down there. I screamed and he ran away."

Firefighters agreed that arson was the cause and did not question her tale of the unknown "pervert" who set her home ablaze. Blanche would take the proceeds from the fire insurance and purchase a mobile home.

A month later, however, the mobile home was burned to the ground. Blanche once again blamed a "pervert" whom she said followed her to the trailer home. The authorities believed her and she collected another fire insurance check.

"Really not sure what Blanche was doing with all this money," Orange said. "She had to have over a quarter of a million dollars on hand from inheritances and sexual harassment suits. She soon realized that money could be gained quicker through settlements as opposed to hard work."

Still on the lookout for a "new man," Blanche met the acquaintance of the Reverend Dwight Moore on Easter Sunday of 1985.

Moore was the pastor of the Carolina United Church of Christ. Divorced with two grown children of his own, the fifty-one-year-old preacher immediately caught the eye of the forty-two-year-old Blanche.

She introduced herself at the end of his sermon and complimented him on his speaking ability. He soon began "counseling" her as her impending lawsuit with Kroger came to a head.

The two got to know each other and Blanche was judgmental toward the Reverend when she found out that his own marriage ended when he was discovered to have an affair with another woman in his church. But Moore was taken by the beauty and Southern charm of Blanche and would not be denied.

"Moore saw Blanche as the innocent victim," Orange said. "She could do no wrong in his eyes and this blinded him to a lot of things, mainly the fact that she had instigated the flirtation and was still involved with Reid. And oh yeah, she just killed her husband. But Blanche saw opportunity in the Reverend. The preacher man was divorced and the pastor of a relatively small church. So she probably saw authority in that. She liked men in the authority, whether it be a manager at Kroger's or a man giving a sermon in a small church."

It began platonic enough, at first, the two began meeting for lunch then dinner on a "friends" basis. Blanche did begin dropping hints that they shouldn't be surprised if she married a "preacher man" in the near future.

"The Reverend was putty in the hands of a seductress like Blanche," Orange said. "Blanche could quote scripture then talk explicitly about sex. She put up a false front of a churchgoing woman but had a carnal way about her. The Reverend took one look at her and thought to himself 'we got a live one here!'"

Moore was smitten and his phone calls to Blanche increased over time. He would leave notes on Blanche's front door step which were sometimes intercepted by Blanche's daughters.

The Reverend would invite Blanche out to "get some ice cream" and the two would soon arrive together as church gatherings.

"She was dating both both the Reverend Moore and Raymond Reid," Orange said. "Her daughters believed that her relationship with Reid had cooled off but nobody told Raymond. Moore seemed none the wiser that Blanche was still seeing Reid. So Blanche was playing both sides against the other. If things worked out with the Reverend she would dump Reid."

Reid would not go away easy. He had abandoned his own wife over twelve years earlier in the hopes of eventually marrying Blanche.

"She couldn't just break-up with Reid," Orange said. "She was in too deep. She got to know his family and friends. The expectation was that they were going to get married but for whatever reason in Blanche's mind, she held out. So, rather than string him along further she decided to eliminate him from the equation."

Reid came down with a case of the "shingles" in 1986 as he developed a skin condition that would point to arsenical peripheral neuritis.

By April, he would be hospitalized with the same symptoms as Blanche's previous victims. This would include diarrhea, projectile vomiting and a loss of sensation in both his hands and feet.

Again, physicians dropped the ball in assessing these classic warning signs of arsenic poisoning. The doctors ordered special tests for "heavy metals intoxication" as well as a urine test which showed six times the normal amount of arsenic in Reid's system.

The report never reached the desk of the doctor's and Reid would continue to suffer.

Blanche would play the role of the dutiful girlfriend but again her inappropriate comments would be put on display when on occasion Reid's son Steve left the room with an attractive young woman. When the young man returned, Blanche asked: "Well, did you fuck her?"

The young man looked on in shock then denied the accusation.

"Well, why not? Growing boy your age needs some pussy once in a while. What's the last time you had some good pussy?"

DEVOTED GIRLFRIEND

When she wasn't harassing Reid's young son, Blanche would be by the side of the sick man on a daily basis. She put on a false front to Reid and his nurses, quoting the Bible and giving the impression that she was a compassionate, Christian woman attending to the needs of her boyfriend.

"She made quite an impression on the nurses on duty," Orange said. "They would testify later that she was the epitome of the caring girlfriend. She showed the man compassion and caring and the all thought that he was very lucky to have Blanche Taylor Moore in his life."

Reid would be diagnosed with Guillain-Barre Syndrome, an auto-immune disorder with the symptoms being muscle weakness, nerve-tingling and progressive fatigue.

"Raymond would die and be revived again," Orange said. "His heart failed and he would be declared clinically dead, losing heartbeat and respiration but the medical staff was able to revive him."

Blanche, however, would be waiting to provide "care" after the staff saved her boyfriend's life. She would come with a cup of processed food and eagerly feed Reed after his latest return from the dead. She would make a show of giving Reid her homemade pudding and specially made "milkshakes".

"Her demeanor was so sweet and unassuming that the nurses wouldn't even think of questioning her," Orange said. "They would nurse Reid back to health, get some of that poison out of his system then Blanche would come into the room with her 'concoctions.' It was literally one step forward and ten steps back for the poor man."

Raymond would recuperate then relapse again into respiratory arrest.

"Think of the worst flu you've ever had then multiply it by ten," Orange said. "Then you're resuscitated again and again. He was on a roller coaster for his life. Absolutely horrific. All the while, Blanche would witness Reid's battles with death. She knew she was the cause of it, with her arsenic milkshakes and pudding, yet she would stand there aghast, praying to the God above that Reid be delivered from the illness."

Reid would regain consciousness but remain confused. He would then began to recuperate and get his senses back. He would feel optimistic about his chances then he would relapse again.

Physical and psychological torture on repeat play.

This would continue for three months. Blanche seized the opportunity to have Reid create a living will. She named herself as executor and beneficiary to one-third of Reid's estate. The other two-thirds would be divided between his sons.

"Blanche had a way about her," Orange said. "She could talk just about any man into doing anything for her. A great deal of her ability to have gotten away with the things she did was her own persona. By this time, she had killed her father, first husband, and her mother-in-law with the exact same methods. Yet no one ever suspected anything or put two and two together, not even those closest to her. Her persona was so ingratiating and unassuming that it would be unthinkable."

After the will was drawn out, Reid's health rapidly deteriorated. In October of 1986, he was brought into intensive care suffering from renal and respiratory failure. He would die three days later as his body began bloating so severely that his skin ripped apart.

According to her daughters, Blanche seemed torn up that Reid had passed away.

Doctor's blamed Guillain-Barre syndrome but wanted an autopsy to be certain. Blanche declined, manipulating Reid's sons into agreeing with her that no autopsy be performed.

"Blanche was like most serial killers," Orange said. "Narcissistic. She thought she was special. She thought she was smarter than everyone else and that she would never be caught."

This now opened the door to a relationship with the Reverend Moore.

"The coast was clear," Orange said.

The Reverend accompanied Blanche to Reid's funeral. She had acquired over $30,000 from Redis's estate in addition to pilfering his safe deposit box and the safe in his home. Reid's sons also gave Blanche over $45,000 from their father's life insurance in the belief that "he would have wanted it that way."

"Then the Reverend didn't waste any time," Orange said. "After an obligatory period of grieving, the Reverend pursued her with great fervor until she finally relented and the two had a wedding date set for August of 1987, less than ten months after Reid's death. Blanche now had a sizable nest egg but most likely lost it all through audacious spending and mismanagement. She had money acquired from the sexual harassment suit, her first husband, and now money gained through her manipulation of Reid's will. She got addicted to the scheming. The game playing and manipulation. It was all an adrenaline rush to her."

THE PERFECT WOMAN

To Moore's family and friends, Blanche seemed like the perfect woman for him. She put on a front of knowing the Bible backward and forwards, having the personality of a "church lady" to match.

"Behind the scenes," Orange said. "Both the Reverend and Blanche knew better. She was a hot number to be sure and everything that was repressed in the Reverend now came to fore. He would now have his cake and eat it too, the Southern man's dream of having a woman who is a lady in church but a tiger in bed."

Things were looking rosy until Blanche was diagnosed with breast cancer. She had one breast surgically removed in order to stop the spread. She went into recovery and the couple pushed the marriage ceremony back another year, to November 27th, 1988.

Things were still not meant to be, however, as three weeks before the wedding the Reverend Moore came down with a mysterious illness all his own. He suffered from vomiting and diarrhea so severe that he had to be hospitalized. Doctors would discover an "intestinal blockage" in the preacher and he was forced to undergo surgery.

Blanche and the Reverend were finally able to tie the knot in April of 1989.

The wedding was simple and witnessed by only two church members.

"She had on a real pretty dress," Doris Pender said, one of the witnesses. "They were beaming. It seemed like there was electricity there. It seemed like they were very much in love."The two lovebirds would go to Montclair, New Jersey for their honeymoon and also visit the Reverend Moore's first grandchild who had just been born.

The honeymoon would be short-lived as the Reverend Moore collapsed on a homeward bound trip five days later.

"There are two competing stories," Orange said. "One is that he ate a pastry then collapsed. The other is that he was spraying insect repellent on some flowers outside his home. Blanche came back with a chicken sandwich for him which promptly made the Reverend sick."

The symptoms eventually grew worse and the Reverend insisted on going to the hospital. He was admitted to the Alamance County Hospital on April 28th and his conditioned worsened after Blanche delivered some "homemade soup."

The doctors inexplicably sent him home but Moore's condition would worsen after he consumed another one of Blanche's meals. She would then drive him to North Carolina Memorial hospital which refused admittance without a written order from Alamance County.

The Reverend had now retained forty pounds of body fluid while Blanche got the necessary paperwork. She would then relay to the Reverend's family that he "was fine, we're just going to do some tests."

Moore's symptoms mirrored that of Guillain-Barre syndrome, the medical staff became suspicious because of the speed of which the symptoms appeared.

"This go around the medical staff tested him for arsenic poisoning," Orange said. "They found huge doses of the poison in his system and immediately suspected that Blanche had given it to him."

The Reverend fought back successfully against the poison. He was able to recuperate and was released from the hospital.

"Reverend Moore set a medical record," Orange said. "The physicians on duty noted that he had survived a dosage of arsenic higher than anyone on record. There was enough poison to kill a moose. Yet the Reverend survived. Amazing."

The police were summoned and became suspicious when they began investigating the number of people associated with Blanche that had died under similar circumstances.

"She didn't do anything," the Reverend Moore said when asked by the police if he believed that Blanche was to blame for his illness. "No way. Not my Blanche. I think I must have inhaled poison while I was spraying the garden for pests."

But the police saw a pussy-whipped man when they saw one. They proceeded to question Blanche who would deny bringing any food to Raymond Reid while he was hospitalized. The claim was contradicted by hospital staffers who were on hand to witness Blanche force Reid to drink one of her "homemade milkshakes."

Investigating further, authorities found out that Blanche had tried to get the Reverend's pension revised so that she would be the principal beneficiary. Blanche became worried that they would test the Reverend for arsenic poison. She had her husband's hair shaved bald but investigating officials were able to obtain samples from the Reverend's pubic region and tested that.

"Both Dwight (Reverend Moore) and Raymond felt depressed," Blanche said when asked why both of her lovers tested high for arsenic. "They were probably taking arsenic themselves."

Police would charge Blanche with assault and had the body of Reid exhumed on his body, consistent with those found on the body of her first husband, James Taylor.

The chief medical examiner would discover that Reid's illness was not only the cause of arsenic but that he continued to receive the poison while he was in the hospital.

The Reverend would refuse to believe that his wife would do such a thing. It took six weeks but the police finally convinced him otherwise after they exhumed the bodies of Raymond Reid and James Taylor.

"You're lucky," the detective informed him. "Damn lucky you're even alive."

The Reverend then confronted Blanche about the accusations he heard from the police. He informed her that their marriage was over. The decision was an emotionally devastating one for the Reverend as Blanche left his hospital bedside covered in crocodile tears.

MOTIVATION?

The townsfolk and those close to Blanche immediately wanted to know why. Why would such a sweet and unassuming woman commit such diabolical crimes. The district attorney, however, couldn't care less. He just knew that the crimes had taken place.

"We don't have to get into why," the DA said. "When you start looking for a rational motive, you generally start overthinking. I just know that this guy died and the state medical examiner said he had a fatal level of arsenic in him."

Blanche was arrested and charged with the murder of Raymond Reid which the DA felt would be easier to prove than the Reverend's poisoning.

During the trial, which opened in Winston-Salem on October 21st, 1990, Blanche continued to deny giving Reid any food. The state produced over fifty-three witnesses who contradicted her statement. Reid's ex-wife and sons also sued Baptist Hospital for malpractice.

During her trial, jurors would discover how Blanche would kill her victims with kindness. She would place the arsenic in the food she would bring for him until ultimately he died.

"Raymond Reid lay in Baptist Hospital flat on his back, bed sores on his back, completely unable to move, tears in his eyes on the days that this woman who was killing him doesn't come," lead prosecutor Janet Branch told the jury, tears streaming down her face.

"He's crying because his murderer isn't coming to see him! Can you imagine anything more pitiful in this whole world? And he loves her with all his heart. ... But she's running around on him, and she's sleeping with Dwight Moore, and she's going to that hospital."

"I never felt the need for vengeance," Moore said. "I have no desire to see her executed. I don't even object to her efforts to get off death row. I have no feelings against her living out her final days in the most humane way possible."

"The authorities began to realize that they had a serial killer on their hands," Orange said. "They wanted to exhume the bodies of everyone that knew Blanche Taylor Moore in their lives. There was a bit of a hysteria going on. Ultimately, I think the authorities decided not to pursue the matter beyond what they could prove in court. The countless one night stands by Blanche would have been impossible to track considering her tenure at Kroger's."

They would exhume five bodies. Traces of arsenic were found in the bodies of both her first husband and her father.

She was cleared of any wrongdoing in her father's death but many believed that the trauma she suffered at the hands of her father led to her becoming a serial killer.

"Her father was a womanizer," Orange said. "And he had abandoned the family had some point. I think that perhaps she mirrored his behavior in her own life and took it a step further, taking out revenge on her father with the many men she came into contact with."

"It certainly isn't uncommon for female serial killers to carry bad relationships with their father into their future relationships with men."

"She is killing her father over and over again."

"I have no doubts as to her guilt," the Reverend Moore said. "The worst lingering effect has been tremors in my hands and weakness in my legs along with peripheral neuropathy. My feet and legs are pretty much a constant reminder (of Blanche).

Blanche Taylor Moore remains on death row in North Carolina. She is the oldest inmate on death row in the state.

TAMMY DUVALL

When Alan Duvall died in August of 2007, his family wasn't satisfied with the initial explanation. Three years later, their doubts were put to rest when authorities arrested his estranged wife, Tami, and charged her with murder, insurance fraud, and obstruction of justice.

According to Bartholomew County prosecutors, Tami was hoping to cash in on a life insurance policy that had been taken out on her husband in the amount of $100,000 – and she decided to poison her husband using stolen medications.

A good catch

Tami was a divorcée in her late 40s when she met Alan – but she didn't look it. Despite having three teenagers, Tami still took pride in her appearance. She wore makeup every day, wore her hair carefully styled, and dressed in nice clothing. And, according to Detective Marc Kruchten, she'd been "medically enhanced," with breast implants, a tummy tuck, and more.

"She was very attractive – she could fix herself up to be a knockout," said Don Engleman, who had been married to Tami previously. "She was what they called a good catch, according to the people in the area – a looker, as they said."

And according to her friend and neighbour, Jennifer Melton, Tami was also very generous and thoughtful.

"There was one Christmas where I was a little short on money and my kids were younger, and she left $300 for my kids," she said. "Tami seemed like a really great person, a really great friend."

It was Jennifer who introduced Tami to ex-Navy Seal Alan Duvall. She felt the two had "matching personalities" – both friendly, outgoing, and kind. Alan was also attractive, and didn't look to be in his mid-fifties.

"He was the type of guy who, when he walked in the room, you turned around and noticed – you noticed him," said Maribeth Kahle, one of Alan's ex girlfriends.

Other friends pointed to Alan's confidence, and his ability to make people feel positive and upbeat. But he hadn't dated in a while, and was lonely and seeking companionship – someone to connect with. And he seemed to have more to offer than just good looks and a sparkling personality.

"If you looked at Alan, he looked rich," said Zillah Thompson, Alan's cousin. "The way he carried himself, the clothes he wore, the jewelry he wore – he looked rich."

According to Maria Williams, a friend of Alan's, Tami had likely been attracted to Alan's potential bank account – or at least, what she suspected his account might look like. However, according to David Thompson, Alan's cousin, he wasn't wealthy at all.

"After he got out of the Navy, he worked on the oil field, I think, out in Oklahoma or somewhere out west," he said.

But Alan was juggling a number of jobs to keep up with his lavish lifestyle. He also did landscaping, worked in a jewelry store, and worked as a maintenance man at a local hotel – which provided him with a place to live, rent-free.

"Everyone was really happy for them, because they seemed really in love, and very, very happy," said Jennifer, "so we were all like, this is great."

Just weeks after Tami and Alan met, he proposed – he'd found the woman he loved, and he planned to be with her for the rest of his life. While many of their friends felt the relationship had progressed too quickly, they tried to be happy for the new couple.

"She wanted a honeymoon, and she wanted to go to Hawaii," said Zillah.

And so, they went – on Tami's line of credit. They had a great time, according to friends, but when the honeymoon ended, she expected

Alan to reimburse her for what she'd spent on the trip. She also demanded that he move out of the hotel, where he lived for free, and buy a house with her. A bigger home, in a nicer neighbourhood.

"He knew it was over his means, and it was over her means – they both knew it," Zillah added. "But he did it for her."

Though Tami seemed to have Alan wrapped around her finger, there was one thing about him that she was unable to control. He liked to drink, and it was becoming a problem for her. She would beg him not to drink, but he didn't seem to be able to resist.

"This is man who drank very often – every time I saw him, he had a beer in his hand," Maria said.

To deal with some of her mounting frustrations, Tami started hitting the mall. Although she'd kept her own secret bank account, her income wasn't enough to cover the bills she was racking up on clothes – some she never even took out of her closet.

"She would get it under control for a little bit, and then, she'd turn right back around and start over again," said her ex-husband, Don.

Just one year into their marriage, the couple started bickering regularly. According to Jennifer, they were "doing a lot more fighting than anything else." Tami's family owned a substantially sized farm, which she'd told Alan she would eventually inherit – and with that in mind, Alan made every effort to make the relationship work.

But Tami caught the eye of the son of one of her favorite patients – and soon after, she and insurance agent Gary Ruddell started seeing each other on the side. When Alan found out about the affair, he decided to fight back in the way he knew would hurt Tami the most.

"Alan closed their joint bank account, and opened a bank account solely in his name," said Detective Marc Kruchten.

And when Tami received a call from her youngest daughter claiming Alan had hit her while he was drinking, she reported to the police that he was drunk and violent. But the officers who responded to the call found no marks on Tami's daughter, and no charges were filed.

After Alan had spent the night at a hotel at the request of the authorities, he returned home to find that the locks on the house had been changed. The couple's separation had officially begun – within days of their second wedding anniversary.

Alan wasn't willing to give up on his marriage, however.

"I think that Alan truly loved Tami – and when you truly love someone, it's hard to cut that off," Maria said.

When Tami invited Alan over to sign what she said were papers related to mortgage insurance, she told him she would consider letting him move back in after her daughter left for college. And, to show him how serious she was about her renewed interest in their marriage, she asked him to come over for a home cooked dinner.

"She said that she was encouraging Alan to go home, and he said he would later – and he was drinking, he was drinking quite heavily," said Detective Marc Kruchten. "When she realized it was time for her to go to bed, Alan was still out there."

When she got up for work and looked out the window, she saw that Alan's truck was still parked in front of the house. He'd passed out in the backyard, and when she tried to wake him up to send him to work, he told her he'd get up on his own, later.

But when she came back after her shift, she found him unresponsive in the chair. And by the time paramedics arrived, it's too late for CPR – Alan is dead.

Accidental alcohol poisoning

Tami told the police that he'd been by her home the evening prior, to help her repair a malfunctioning air conditioning unit. He was a heavy sleeper, she said, and since she'd moved out, he'd taken to drinking heavily and passing out on the back porch, outside. He'd also become overheated while he'd been working on her air conditioner, she added, and he'd been feeling depressed that she'd moved out of their house and the couple were no longer living together.

Initially, investigators determined that the death was due to accidental alcohol poisoning, combined with heat exhaustion from the significant amount of time Alan had spent outside that day. Tami was adamant that her husband had likely just drank himself to death, and a test revealed that his blood alcohol level was 0.436 percent – well above the legal limit.

"However, several of [Tami] and Alan's family members contacted the Columbus Police Department to convey their suspicions of foul play," stated court documents, "prompting Detective Marc Kruchten to request an autopsy of Alan's body."

But Tami tried to prevent an autopsy being done on Alan's body, claiming she wanted to move on with the cremation as soon as possible – despite the fact that her husband had already purchased a burial plot well in advance of his demise. It was that autopsy that would reveal the presence of the additional drugs in his system, the muscle relaxer and the lethal dose of morphine.

Additional screening indicated his blood also contained approximately 100 times the maximum therapeutic level of morphine, court records stated, as well as approximately eight times a therapeutic dose of muscle relaxer. And while Alan's stepbrother, Henry McCune, admitted his brother enjoyed the drink, he was suspicious when he heard that the tests had also revealed the presence of drugs.

"Both of us never believed in drugs," he told The Republic newspaper in 2010. "If somebody walked in his house and had drugs, he would throw them out."

Digging deeper

In light of the new information provided by the toxicology report, Detective Kruchten opened a homicide investigation.

According to court documents, the detective's investigation immediately revealed significant financial issues faced by the couple.

"Creditors were continually calling the marital residence to discuss delinquencies of various consumer accounts and past-due vehicle payments," the documents read. "The marital residence was a subject of foreclosure proceedings, and college tuition for [Tami's] youngest daughter had become due."

Following a number of job changes, Alan had recently started working with a glass installation company, and Tami's income as a certified nurse's aide at Miller's Merry Manor wasn't enough to cover the couple's mounting financial obligations. Still, Tami seemed to blame her husband for their money troubles – she'd often complained to those around her, including friends, co-workers, and her daughter, that Alan was "unreliable," and failed to provide adequate contributions to the family's finances.

Acquaintances told police they believed Tami had been having an affair with the insurance agent who had drafted Alan Duvall's policy. The couple's marital problems were becoming progressively worse, and Tami had apparently gotten involved with someone else.

According to witnesses who knew the couple, Tami had been saying that she intended to file for divorce – but that she'd managed to persuade Alan to list her as the beneficiary on his life insurance policy by convincing him that they would eventually reconcile. Just one month before Alan died, the policy – which had been filled out by hand – was signed in front of a restaurant in Columbus.

While the insurance situation had already raised red flags, Alan's family's suspicions grew when it appeared that Tami was attempting to rush the cremation process and skip past the autopsy. According to Henry, she seemed anxious to get it over with quickly.

"I was suspicious of it at the start," he admitted. "He was in too good of health."

In Tami's own affidavit, her story about the circumstances of her husband's death shifted. Initially, she implied to police that he'd probably drank himself to death – she'd come home, found him unconscious, and immediately dialed 911. But this original account was proven to be false after testimony was collected from witnesses.

Shockingly forgetful

According to the clerk of a local convenience store, Kim Foster, Tami had been acting strangely when they'd spoken briefly that morning, before she had opened the store at around 7 am. When Kim asked Tami if everything was alright, she testified that Tami told her she'd just been to her house, where she'd found her husband dead.

After speaking with the clerk, witness accounts revealed Tami went back to the house and knocked on the door of her next door neighbour, Jennifer Melton, at approximately 7 am. Melton stated that she went to answer the door to see what Tami needed, but by the time she reached her front entry, Tami had already gone. When she looked out the back door, toward the Duvalls' home, she saw Tami in the backyard, tying up her dogs.

Gary Ruddell had also spoken to Tami that morning. At around 7:30, he testified, she'd phoned to tell him that she'd found Alan outside on the back porch, and that he was "unconscious."

According to authorities, Tami asked on several occasions when the department planned to close the investigation, as it was hampering her efforts to secure the amount of Alan's life insurance policy.

After authorities confronted Tami with this conflicting information, she admitted it was possible she had made a few other calls before she dialed 911 – blaming her poor memory of the morning and unusual reaction on the "shock" she'd experienced after finding her husband's body.

According to what Tami had originally told detectives, she'd been making drinks for Alan the night before he died, while he was at her house repairing the air conditioner. At that time, she'd claimed to have served him at least two Long Island iced teas. However, during a conversation with Alan's ex wife, Mary, Tami initially said Alan hadn't been drinking at all – but later, mentioned that during the course of the evening, he'd consumed one beer and one shot. And when she spoke with one of the couple's children, Tami said Alan had been pounding tequila the entire night.

And despite what Tami had first told police, that she believed Alan had accidentally drunk himself to death, she eventually changed that story, too. She told investigators that Alan had actually made the decision to drink the morphine all on his own. According to Tami, he drank the medication and swallowed the pills because "he wasn't willing to live if he couldn't move back home and have free reign to do the things he wanted to do."

Court documents state that early in the police investigation, Tami suggested to authorities that her husband had – contrary to what his friends and relatives had reported – been a drug user in the past. He'd even "hid the other part of his life" from her deliberately, she'd claimed, but could provide no specific knowledge about what drugs he might have taken or how he had used them.

In an interview with Detective Kruchen and Bartholomew County Prosecutor William Nash, she alleged to have seen her husband take Flexeril brand muscle relaxers, which she said he told her were obtained from his cousin, Zillah Thompson.

"Thompson admitted that she had left medications, including Flexeril, out in plain view at her house, and that she had recently had a block party attended by the Duvalls," court documents read. "However, those who knew Alan, including Thompson, insisted that Alan was opposed to ingesting drugs."

Additionally, Tami said, on the night before Alan's death, she'd seen him with an eye dropper bottle filled with what appeared to be a lavender colored liquid – a description police said was consistent with Roxanol, a liquid form of morphine commonly prescribed to hospice patients. She also admitted to police that, after she'd found Alan's body, she'd disposed of what she said were empty medication and alcohol bottles from their home.

"Police officers testified that neither Roxanol nor Flexeril was a drug typically abused or available for street purchase," stated court documents. "Evidence showed that [Tami] had been in the proximity of both drugs shortly before Alan's death."

Increasing concern

Prior to his death, Alan had been growing more and more concerned about his own well being. In the weeks and months leading up to the murder, he'd warned his friends and neighbours that if he was found dead, to ensure the case was thoroughly investigated – he worried his estranged wife might consider offing him.

Both Tami's previous ex-husband and her own daughter confessed to police that they, too, believed Tami was responsible for Alan's murder.

It took the police three years to put the case together, but eventually, they determined Tami had put the morphine and muscle relaxers into her husband's pudding – and after she was charged and held with no bail, a court case got underway.

The major hurdle for Tami's defense was explaining to the court how Alan ended up with morphine in his system. It was well documented among Alan's family and friends that he liked to drink, but no one seemed willing to believe that he'd knowingly use drugs – prescription, or otherwise.

There was also evidence that Tami had stolen the narcotics from the nursing home where she'd been working at the time. In March of 2007, the facility had documented that an almost full bottle of liquid morphine – Roxanol – had gone missing. And according to the nurse who had originally noticed the disappearance, Charles Rose, Tami had been the only person anywhere near the area at that time.

"As a certified nurse's aide, [Tami] was not permitted authorized access to patient drugs, and so the State necessarily alleged a theft," court documents read. "Rose testified that [Tami] was working with him on March 2, 2007, on a particular ward that housed a hospice patient who had been prescribed Roxanol."

Another nurse's aide, Rita Bell, had been on duty with Charles and Tami. Charles went for lunch with Rita, according to court documents, and left Tami alone on the floor to serve lunches to the bedridden patients.

"Bell had seen a bottle of Roxanol on a patient's table, but did not pick it up because she was not in charge of the medicine cart on that day," the documents continued.

When Charles had asked Tami if she knew what happened to it, he told the court, Tami had flatly denied having taken it, and blamed the missing drugs on a relative of a patient the nurse said hadn't been on the floor that day.

"According to Rose, he 'kind of knew better,' because the daughter was a teacher who never visited during the daytime," read court documents.

However, according to Tami, the testimony provided by Charles Rose that she "stole liquid morphine from Miller's Merry Manor is tenuous at best." Instead, she pointed to testimony provided by Robyn Sams, director of nursing at the facility, who had told the court that she "decided to mark the bottle as spilled" and said there was no way to prove where the drugs had ended up.

And, since pathologist Dr. Greg Brown testified for the jury that the official cause of Alan Duvall's death had been an overdose of morphine, the evidence was admitted to show the jury that Tami had had easy access to the weapon used in her husband's murder.

"The value of evidence that [Tami] had access to the murder weapon, a rare form of morphine typically used for palliative care for dying patients, was high," read court documents. "Moreover, the access had been in recent proximity to Alan's death."

Habitual behaviour

Other challenging testimony came from Alan's family and friends. They told the court that although the couple were estranged, they were still facing significant challenges together, primarily financial ones. The home was going into foreclosure, and Alan told them he'd recently signed "mortgage insurance" on the property – but the only policy the couple had purchased in the months prior to Alan's death was his life insurance.

Alan's friends also believed that he was in the process of reconciling with his estranged wife, that Tami had told him she planned to move back into the marital home as soon as her youngest daughter went off to college. But according to Tami's friends and family, she'd told them there was no reconciliation in their future – in fact, in her testimony to the court, Rhonda Brown said Tami had told her she had no plans to get back together with Alan because she was still trying to pursue a relationship with Gary Ruddell.

Questionable activities from Tami's past were also brought up during the trial. While investigating Tami's involvement in Alan's death – and the potential insurance fraud she was intending to commit – detectives learned that she'd previously reported a theft to her insurance company at that time.

According to court documents, Tami had apparently accused an ex boyfriend of stealing her property. When police tracked down Tami's former boyfriend, Stephen Brown, he denied having stolen anything, and informed them that he'd had concerns about Tami that sounded eerily familiar.

Stephen told authorities that he believed Tami had tried to poison him sometime around Thanksgiving of 2004 – and that after her first attempt, she began persuading him to sign new life insurance documents. According to Stephen's story, Tami had stopped by his house with some food. It was pudding, she told him, made by her daughter especially for him. Stephen ate the dessert, but confessed he thought it "tasted like aspirin" and made him feel "out of it" for the next few hours.

Just after the incident, he said, Tami had provided him with a stack of paperwork she wanted him to sign – a life insurance policy, according to Stephen, that would make Tami the beneficiary. When he refused to fill out the papers, she left Stephen's house, taking with her the bowl and plate she'd brought the tainted meal on.

Gary Ruddell, the insurance salesman Tami had allegedly been sleeping with, was never implicated in the murder. He also claimed he knew nothing about any potential plan Tami had been concocting regarding the crime.

At her trial, however, he testified that he had advised that she not attempt to collect on the recently purchased life insurance policy following Alan's death – according to Gary, the policy was still in its "grace period" and would likely arouse suspicion. Tami refused to heed Gary's warnings, and an investigator was eventually assigned to the case by the insurance company.

The agent, Dennis Thomas, would end up joining forces with the local police, investigating the circumstances surrounding the death of Alan Duvall.

Jury deliberations began on the tenth day of the trial, but it only took the jurors six hours to return with a verdict. On April 22, 2011, Tami Duvall was found guilty on all counts – six counts of insurance fraud, three counts of obstruction of justice, and murder. Just one month later, she was handed down a prison sentence of more than six decades behind bars.

"[Tami's] convictions for insurance fraud stem from six false statements given in a single insurance investigation interview on May 29, 2008," read court documents. "Her three convictions for obstruction of justice stem from a single crime scene clean-up (in which she removed an alcohol bottle, medication container, and foam from Alan's mouth) on August 24, 2007."

Tami appealed the conviction and the sentence in 2012, but the court refused to budge on the murder conviction. While that charge was upheld, the counts for the insurance fraud and obstruction of justice were all lowered – and according to the Department of Corrections, her sentence was reduced to 55 years for the murder conviction, four years for the insurance fraud, and 1.5 years for obstruction of justice.

"The trial court did not commit reversible error or fundamental error in the admission of evidence, and therefore we affirm the murder conviction," read the judge's opinion. "However, because [Tami's] acts constitute a single chargeable offense under the continuing crime doctrine, we affirm one conviction each for insurance fraud and obstruction of justice, but reverse and remand with instructions to vacate the five remaining convictions for insurance fraud and the remaining two convictions for obstruction of justice."

With her earliest possible release delayed until 2040, Tami Duvall will likely die while incarcerated – a fitting punishment for someone who had hoped to live carefree thanks to the deaths of others.

JASMINE RICHARDSON

GERTRUDE SCOTT

On the South Saskatchewan River in Alberta, Canada is a town called Medicine Hat. With a population of just over 60,000 it is filled with little communities where everybody knows everybody. With a relatively low crime rate and virtually none of those crimes involving homicide it's the perfect place to raise a family in a safe environment, or at least it would seem that way I should I say. The security offered by Medicine Hat was greatly diminished when the entire town was shaken to its core in April of 2006.

On April 23, 2006 the community was rocked to its very foundation with the discovery of a gruesome triple homicide. An entire family was found stabbed to death in their home that day. The bodies were discovered by the 8 year old boy's best friend when he arrived at the house to get his friend to come out and play. When cops were notified and an investigation began the scene revealed was one of the worst scenes in Canadian history. Debra Richardson, 48 and her husband Marc, 42 were found in the basement with multiple stab wounds covering their bodies and upon further investigation their son 8 year old Jacob was found also stabbed to death with his throat slit in his bed upstairs. Such a horrific scene was left behind that the police responding would be affected long after the investigation. It didn't take police long to realize that family photos around the home depicted a family of 4 instead of 3. The 12 year old daughter Jasmine was missing. Immediately police were concerned that they had a kidnapping on their hands. The sweet angelic looking daughter in the photos must have been victimized by the monster that did this to her family as well. However, the sweet loving family photos that the police encountered depicting a 12 year old girl were not the reality where Jasmine was concerned. Jasmine had started acting and dressing differently. She had new friends, she was getting in trouble and going off to wild parties and she had a 23 year old boyfriend that her parents detested here being with. That boyfriend was into drugs, drinking, and dark things like werewolves, vampires, and the Goth culture. In fact that boyfriend even claimed to be a werewolf himself and reportedly professed to liking the taste of blood. Jasmine Richardson was not missing because she had been kidnapped rather she was missing because she was responsible. It would be later discovered that Jasmine and her 23 year old boyfriend, Jeremy Steinke had committed the murders themselves and had gone on the run.

Background

Once upon a time Jasmine Richardson was the sweet little girl depicted in the family photos around the Richardson house. Once upon a time the family was the perfect poster family for suburban bliss but something went wrong. Jasmine became interested in the Goth culture as well as the Wiccan religion. With this interest came a dark side to the little girl.

At 12 the little girl looked much older; perhaps 15 or 16 and she even claimed to be that old on social media. Soon she had the attention of local man Jeremy Steinke. Jasmine and Jeremy fell into a dangerous relationship. They idolized a life of negativity. They dressed in dark fantasy type clothing and they frequented sites on the internet like vampire freaks, a social media site for teens that love all things vampire. In fact Jeremy himself claimed to love the taste of blood and that he was a 300 year old werewolf. Jeremy had more practice at the twisted lifestyle that they both began to lead than Jasmine did but he was also weakened by a controlling effect that Jasmine had on him. Jasmine knew how to manipulate Jeremy. In many ways this seemed to spell love for Jeremy; he had found a girl that he would do anything for. In Jasmine's case Jeremy was an adult that she could control. She might have to live under what felt like the tyranny of her parents and she might have to go by the rules at the strict Catholic school that she attended but with Jeremy she had the say so. She could only wish for something and Jeremy was there to try to make her wishes come true. This might all sound like the musings of a warped but innocent mind, a reality created by dissatisfied kids looking to feel like they have more control over their lives but Jasmine and Jeremy took things much farther than most kids would dare to go. Just like any good loving parents the Richardsons became alarmed when they learned of the changes in their daughter's lifestyle. The most alarming thing to Jasmine's parents was Jeremy. No parent is going to be comfortable with their 12 year old little girl being in a relationship with a 23 year old man. More alarmingly their relationship was sexual as well. Jasmine may have looked much older but she still had the mind and body of a 12 year old girl chronologically speaking.

When Jasmine told Jeremy online that she had a plan to kill her family he hopped on board. They wrote instant messages to each other discussing the killing of Jasmine's family. Below are the exact words they typed to each other in a snippet of their conversation.

Jasmine: "I have this plan. It begins with me killing them and ends with me living with you."

Jeremy: "I love your plan but we need to get a little more creative with like details and stuff."

Who knows now if either of them were truly serious about committing the murders in the beginning but in the end Jeremy got pumped up watching the movie *Natural Born Killers,* got drunk, did some lines of cocaine and then he was ready to help his beloved carry out her request to alleviate herself of her bothersome parents. All it took was a set of loving protective parents trying to protect their 12 year old daughter from the psychological and perhaps even physical damage that would come from having a sexual relationship with a 23 year old man and Jasmine and Jeremy were all too ready to put an end to the two nuisances trying to keep them apart.

On the night of April 22nd Jeremy watched *Natural Born Killers* with his friends, did some drinking and drugs and then he was ready. He would do anything to make Jasmine happy. Despite her young age and the considerable age gap between the two Jasmine knew how to manipulate Jeremy. Jeremy snuck into the basement of The

Richardson's split level home and waited. Thinking she heard noises Debra Richardson, already in her night gown, went down to investigate. She couldn't have been prepared for what awaited her. As soon as Debra flipped on the light switch Jeremy attacked her stabbing her 12 times before killing her. Debra's husband Marc was close behind after hearing the commotion and armed with a screwdriver. However, in the end his screwdriver was no match for Jeremy's knife. Later Jeremy would tell an undercover police officer that he was worried Marc would get the better of him and that Marc nearly succeeded in defending himself with that screwdriver. No matter the fight Marc put up the scene ended up with him on the floor still in a defensive stance, dead with 24 stab wounds. Later Jeremy would say that Marc asked 'why' just before he died and Jeremy replied, 'it's what your daughter wanted.'

After killing Marc and Debra Jeremy headed upstairs leaving a trail of blood in his wake. Upstairs Jasmine was trying to calm her little brother down. At this point Jeremy and Jasmine's stories are not the same. Both of them say it was the other that actually killed the little boy. I suppose we will never know the truth nevertheless young Jacob was found in his bed with stab wounds in his body and his throat slit side to side. Jasmine and Jeremy left the scene and reportedly went back to a friend's apartment to have sex after obliterating Jasmine's entire family. They were the outlaw lovers that they had dreamed of being bound together even more so by the horrific blood bath they had just caused. The two went on the run but they didn't make it far. After a search of Jasmine's school locker a graphic picture surfaced of a girl's whole family burning in a fire while she laughs and escapes with her boyfriend. When police saw this drawing they went from searching for Jasmine as a victim to searching for her as a suspect.

Jasmine and Jeremy were apprehended in Saskatchewan the very next day after the bodies of her family were discovered. The pair were reportedly laughing and joking around with friends about the murders only one day after they had taken place.

Unfathomable Murder

The Richardsons were the picturesque family living in a picturesque neighborhood. Ross Glen, the community where the Richardsons lived, was a middle class neighborhood full of working class families. Their neighbors on one side were Sara and her six year old son Gareth, Jacob's best friend, and their neighbors on the other side were Phyllis and Vernon Gehring. The Gehrings were an elderly couple that liked to garden and look after their dog, a shi tzu Bishon mix. Often the scene would be that Gareth and Jacob could be found playing in the backyard as children do and the Gehrings would delight in tossing balls back over the fence when they strayed a bit too far. The Gehrings felt like Jacob kept them young. They admittedly didn't know much about the daughter. Just the night before that fateful afternoon when the bodies were found Marc Richardson had grilled hot dogs in the backyard for the boys while the Gehring's dog played with the Richardson family's dog through the fence. Everything seemed perfect in that sleepy little neighborhood until that fateful afternoon on April 23rd when Gareth went looking for his best friend.

It was about 1pm and Sara and Gareth had been at Sara's mom's house but Gareth had been asking to play with Jacob all morning. When Gareth could not get anyone to answer the phone at the Richardson residence Sara told him that they could go to the movies. Gareth was still bummed out about not getting to see Jacob and when he and his mom returned home before heading to the movies he darted over to the Richardson's after seeing that Marc's white pickup truck was in the driveway. Gareth knocked on the door but there was no answer, as a curious little boy might he began peering into the basement windows of the split level home. When he saw lifeless bodies and a basement covered in blood he ran back to his mom to tell her what he'd seen. Although Gareth wasn't usually the type of boy to make up stories the things he was saying to Sara just didn't make sense. As she followed him over to the neighbor's house she warned him that he had better not be lying. Sadly Gareth was not lying. When she peered through the same windows that Gareth had Sara saw a horrible scene in front of her. She was afraid that the intruder that had done this was still around, maybe he was even in her house waiting for her and Gareth. She called her mom and her mom told her she had to call 911. Sara's mom and the police headed to the scene. What would unfold at that crime scene would haunt police officers that investigated for years to come. Some of the officers involved were touched so much by young Jacob's defiled body that they broke down on the stand months later when they had to talk about it.

The police came in thinking that they might have an intruder still lurking about the property. They entered with caution. What they saw was unfathomable. There were the bodies of a man and woman in the basement both covered in blood. The woman, Debra Richardson was slumped in the floor with her night gown hiked up exposing the fact that all she had been wearing when she was attacked was that night gown. There was blood all over her and a pool of blood all around her. The little black family dog was standing beside her. Perhaps he felt that he needed to protect her but sadly it was too late for that. Across the basement slumped against a wall was Marc Richardson. His hands were straight out as though he were trying to defend himself. He was frozen by rigor mortis in a defensive state that did nothing for his defense in the end. Marc was wearing only black boxer shorts and a screwdriver was lying beside him. He, too, was riddled with stab wounds. The entire basement was covered in splatters of blood, there had been a real struggle between the Richardsons and their assailant. Upon further investigation of the house the police came across their worst nightmare. The first bedroom was empty but the next bedroom they came to was Jacob's. Jacob was lying in his bed. Police had hope for a moment that the boy was still alive but when they approached they were greeted with the worst. Jacob was in his bed with his throat slashed and stab wounds littering his body as well. There was blood all over his room including many of his toys. A toy light saber was lying in his floor; a useless object against the onslaught of the knife that had ended his life. In the master bedroom the comforter was thrown back as though the bed's occupants had left in a hurry. There was a pillow thrown awkwardly in the floor. Police wondered with horror if the boy had heard his parents being attacked before the assailant ever made it upstairs to him and clutched the pillow trying to find some comfort in the act. As they made another sweep of the house the police noticed that there were four members of the Richardson family instead of three. Instantly everyone's heart sank. A family photo depicted a sweet smiling 12 year old girl and she was nowhere to be found. Police searched that house several times over for either the body of the little girl or perhaps the girl hiding somewhere too afraid to come out after the horrible things she had witnessed but in the end they had to admit defeat, the fourth member of the Richardson family was nowhere to be seen. On the plus side her body wasn't there slain with the rest of her family but the police had to think the worst. The most logical thought was that she may have been kidnapped by whoever did this to her family. And even if she was safe, perhaps spending the night at a friend's house she would still have to deal with the tragic news that she had no family left, that her family had all been brutally attacked and killed. Hearts went out for the girl and for the family she had lost. No one wanted to be left breaking that news to a 12 year old.

The hunt for Jasmine Richardson began, or actually continued, as her parents had reported that she was missing before the terrible crime had ever even taken place. Where was Jasmine? Safe, but oblivious to the fact that this terrible thing had happened to her parents? Scared alone and possibly seriously injured in the hands of the monster that did this to her family? No one could say. As part of the investigation police visited Jasmine's school and got permission to look inside her locker. They were looking for any kind of evidence that would lead them to Jasmine whatsoever but what they found was truly a shocking discovery. When the police searched Jasmine's locker they found a hand drawn picture depicting a horrible scene. In the picture a girl's family burns to death after she puts gasoline in the sprinklers while they have a family picnic. The stick figure girl in the drawing laughs as her family burns and she escapes in her boyfriend's pickup truck. This drawing shifted suspicions entirely and Jasmine Richardson went from being searched for as a victim to being searched for as a suspect in the murder of her parents and her little brother. Consequently it didn't take the police long to track Jasmine and Jeremy down. The pair were said to be joking around with friends about the murders even at the time of apprehension. They were found at a high school in Saskatchewan only about 60 miles from Medicine Hat.

Both Jasmine and Jeremy were jailed and both were convicted. Because of Jasmine's young age at the time under Canadian law she had to be referred to as JR instead of her name. She also was protected from being tried as an adult. Although she got the maximum sentence for a child her age that sentence was only 10 years and under the conditions the time she had already spent in jail counted toward her 10 years. She ended up being imprisoned under the conditions of 4 years locked up undergoing rehabilitation and 4.5 years under very close supervision in the community. Jeremy, on the other hand, was 23 years old at the time of the murders. He was found guilty of three counts of first degree murder and sentenced to three life sentences to be served consecutively. An undercover officer rode with Jeremy while he was being transported from one facility to the other. In the conversation the two had together Jeremy expressed that he loved Jasmine more than anything and that the kind of thing he did was the kind of thing that truly expressed that love. He admitted to everything he did in such a straight forward way that it seemed he did not even grasp the gravity of the situation. He even shared his plans to marry Jasmine when they were both able to get out of prison. On murderpedia.org you can actually read the transcript of the conversation that Jeremy had with the undercover officer that he believed to be another prison being transported along with him. Steinke will be eligible for parole after 25 years.

Some of the residents of Medicine Hat were actually outraged with the outcome of the trial. They didn't think that justice would be served with Jasmine getting away with such little time. Wayne Chopek is one such resident that has spoken out about his outrage. Wayne was a friend of the family and he is disgusted at the fact that Jasmine would go free after a short ten years. However, the law remains the law and in Canada the government believes that children as young as Jasmine was at the time of the murders need to be rehabilitated rather than being locked up and having the key thrown away. They believe that such young lives have more potential value than to doom them to the rest of their lives behind bars.

Life After Murder

After Jasmine and Jeremy were arrested and jailed they still held onto the flame that was recklessly burning before the murders. They were not able to have any contact with one another except for letter writing so they wrote back and forth. This is how Jeremy came to ask Jasmine to marry him and she said yes. Below is an excerpt of the letters passed between the two when Jeremy popped the question.

Jeremy: "Without you this life isn't worth living... U said you want to get engaged? Then here's a Q...Will U marry me? If so then it is a verbal agreement!"

Jasmine: "Ahahaha! I never thought I'd find myself hystericaly laughing in a holding cell in these kinds of circumstances...or ever really. But still! ahaha you make me so happy! Yes! Yes! I will, I would love to... "

Interestingly enough as bright as that flame might have been it eventually flickered out. Although they professed the deepest of bonds neither of the two would admit to actually being the one to Kill Jacob. Both blamed the other. This was one of the deciding factors that actually showed that there were holes in the loving couple's relationship. The two broke up in jail. After incarceration the relationship that had been important enough to kill for dwindled until it was no more.

Perhaps free of any attachment to Jeremy Steinke Jasmine could truly rehabilitate. Jasmine underwent psychiatric evaluations and was determined to be suffering from oppositional defiance disorder as well as conduct disorder. When she first started therapy she was determined to suffer from dependency issues, anxiety and depression. As well as all this she was prone to immature problem solving and wishful fantasies. All this is a lot to bog down a 12 year old but was it enough of a load to excuse the execution of the murder of her entire family? Many say no, some say yes. At any rate it is indeed enough to at least explain some of her behaviors. Once in therapy Jasmine began making progress toward rehabilitation though in the beginning her details of how things played out her a bit skewed to reality. By 2010 Jasmine was making significant progress in her rehabilitation and had professed to be sorry for the crimes she committed. As the terms of her sentencing were laid out she got credit on her sentence for the time she spent in jail awaiting trial and then after 4 years of incarceration she was deemed fit enough to go into the community under very close supervision for 4.5 years. During that time Jasmine was shown to exhibit exemplary behavior as well as being a straight A student. Jasmine was admitted to Calgary University where she continued to earn really high grades. This year, 2016, in May Jasmine became a completely free woman. The courts have no reason to think that she is a danger to society any longer. It's been a decade and she has been through extensive amounts of therapy and shown nothing but progress in that entire time.

A very interesting thing to look at here is the chemistry between Jasmine and Jeremy. One asks themselves, was the combination just toxic? Would either of them been capable of doing something like this on their own? It seems that the pairing of the two and the dependency that both of them exhibited for the other was actual such an explosive combination that it pushed them over the edge just enough to create the perfect circumstance for this to happen. Jasmine has said that she wasn't really being serious when she would send Jeremy messages saying that she had a plan to kill her parents and live with him. That she didn't really mean to go through with it when she joked about murdering her family or made drawings depicting their deaths. But she felt those feelings and she told Jeremy. Steinke just happened to be easily manipulated, a regular user of multiple drugs, and even believed himself to be a 300 year old werewolf. Jeremy and Jasmine both took the dark Goth culture they lived within to the extreme. They exchanged vials of blood and Jeremy wore one around his neck. When the two were faced with Jasmine's parents making them unable to see one another dark fantasies were transformed into evil realities. Perhaps the fantasies that both harbored were purely fantasies until the tension kept rising and rising and the two kept feeding off of each other until the combination of each of their dark thoughts breathed life into the other. In the end it doesn't really matter to ask if either would have been capable of the atrocity on their own because it wasn't the case that they were on their own. They were bound together by an obsessive unhealthy love and the obsessive unhealthy thoughts in both their heads took form in reality. The result was unspeakable horror.

That late April day three lives were lost much too soon and in such a violent way that it is nearly unthinkable. That alone is enough to make this tragedy stand out forever in history but that's not all that was lost. Little Gareth will never be the same. Though he is a successful high schooler now the memory of those bodies and the memory of the loss of his best friend will always be with him. And of course Jasmine Richardson and Jeremy Steinke's lives will forever be changed and affected. Jeremy will most likely spend his entire life in jail having had only 23 short years of freedom. Parole will be an unlikely event. Even though Jasmine has improved and rehabilitated, even if she successfully integrates back into society, she will forever have this as a part of her past. She will also forever have people that look at her as a monster. Her story is known all over the world. Jasmine is the youngest person in Canada to have ever committed such a heinous crime. It is a question to ponder as to whether Jasmine has forgiven herself or if she is forever haunted by the monster that she perhaps did not even know lurked inside her. Perhaps even scarier to think of is the possibility that she really could live without being constantly haunted by the crime. Is there any amount of rehabilitation that should erase that guilt? And then one has to consider Jeremy. Has he come to terms with the events? Is he sorry for his crimes? Will a life in prison in any way begin to repay his debt for those three lives that he so brutally extinguished?

Life in Medicine Hat continues on. It is still a relatively safe place to live. Medicine Hat is still a relatively small tight knit place filled with working class suburbs. There are still nice neighborhoods that feel safe the way that Ross Glen did before tragedy came to town but no one will forget what could happen no matter how nice or normal a family might seem they will know that a tragedy like this could happen to any family because it already has.